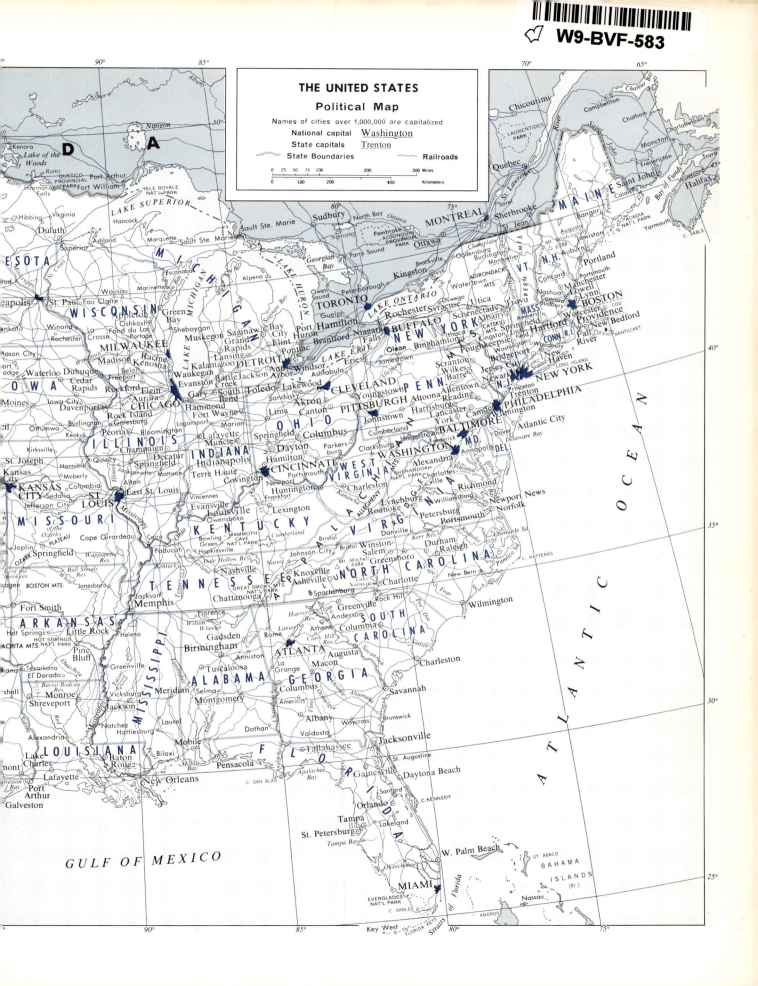

THE UNITED STATES
Political Map

Names of cities over 1,000,000 are capitalized

National capital   Washington
State capitals   Trenton
State Boundaries   Railroads

0 25 50 75 100   200   300 Miles

0   100   200   400
Kilometers

LIFE WORLD LIBRARY

THE UNITED STATES

TIME
LIFE
BOOKS
®

LIFE WORLD LIBRARY

LIFE NATURE LIBRARY

TIME READING PROGRAM

THE LIFE HISTORY OF THE UNITED STATES

LIFE SCIENCE LIBRARY

INTERNATIONAL BOOK SOCIETY

GREAT AGES OF MAN

TIME-LIFE LIBRARY OF ART

TIME-LIFE LIBRARY OF AMERICA

FOODS OF THE WORLD

LIFE WORLD LIBRARY

THE UNITED STATES

by
Patrick O'Donovan
Marcus Cunliffe
Alain Clément
Massimo Salvadori
Sigmund Skard
Peter von Zahn
Max Warren
Herbert von Borch
Raymond Aron
and the Editors of TIME-LIFE BOOKS

TIME-LIFE BOOKS   NEW YORK

COVER: On the Mall in their nation's capital,
Americans stroll beneath the massive,
555-foot shaft of the Washington Monument.
In the foreground are fountains that border
the Rainbow Pool. Beyond, gleaming in the late
afternoon sunlight, rises the white,
colonnaded, cast-iron dome of the Capitol.

Contents

TIME-LIFE BOOKS

EDITOR
Maitland A. Edey
EXECUTIVE EDITOR
Jerry Korn
TEXT DIRECTOR   **ART DIRECTOR**
Martin Mann   Sheldon Cotler
CHIEF OF RESEARCH
Beatrice T. Dobie
PICTURE EDITOR
Robert G. Mason
Assistant Text Directors:
Harold C. Field, Ogden Tanner
Assistant Art Director: Arnold C. Holeywell
Assistant Chief of Research: Martha Turner

•

PUBLISHER
Rhett Austell
Associate Publisher: Walter C. Rohrer
General Manager: Joseph C. Hazen Jr.
Planning Director: John P. Sousa III
Circulation Director: Joan D. Manley
Marketing Director: Carter Smith
Business Manager: John D. McSweeney
Publishing Board: Nicholas Benton,
Louis Bronzo, James Wendell Forbes

LIFE WORLD LIBRARY

SERIES EDITOR: Oliver E. Allen
Editorial Staff for *The United States:*
Assistant Editors: David S. Thomson, Jay Brennan
Designer: Ben Schultz
Chief Researcher: Grace Brynolson
Researchers: Ruth Silva, Helen Muller, Donald Nelson,
Clover Rosenblum, Ellen Youngblood

EDITORIAL PRODUCTION
Color Director: Robert L. Young
Copy Staff: Marian Gordon Goldman, Patricia Miller,
Madge Raymond, Florence Keith
Picture Department: Dolores A. Littles, Barbara Sullivan
Art Assistants: Douglas B. Graham, John M. Woods

The following individuals and departments of Time Inc. gave valuable aid in the preparation of the book: LIFE staff photographers Alfred Eisenstaedt, John Loengard, Leonard McCombe, Francis Miller, Gordon Parks and George Silk; Editorial Production, Robert W. Boyd Jr.; Editorial Reference, Peter Draz; Picture Collection, Doris O'Neil; Photographic Laboratory, George Karas; TIME-LIFE News Service, Richard M. Clurman.

Introduction

Mr. Luce (1898-1967) wrote the following introduction to the first edition of this volume in 1965:

Many readers may not have been aware of one principle that has all along guided the editors of the LIFE World Library in selecting authors for its series. This was that no volume should be written by a national of the country under discussion, and the idea was to establish a cool and consistent series, written by informed outsiders who would be free of nationalist puff or prejudice. Now, in the volume on the United States of America, the editors have asked experts in a number of fields each to do a chapter on his specialty. Following the original rule, all are foreigners, and this time the impact of that rule will probably hit the reader with considerable force.

American readers of this book will, I think, find it, as I did, a rather extraordinary experience. It is like getting a report card from school and finding that you have received much higher marks than you could possibly have expected.

To start with the Economics Department (Professor Massimo Salvadori), perhaps it ought not to be a surprise to be told that the materialistic economic performance of the U.S. is so far ahead of any other society that it is in a class by itself. Surely that is an irrefutable fact known to all. But it is a question whether the miracle of our economic achievement is really appreciated by Americans, both pundits and people. Even if a modern American is aware of this fact, he may still be surprised to find that Professor Salvadori attributes the achievements not primarily to favorable material circumstances but rather to the values and ideals that, generation after generation, have been woven into the American way of life. In our daily business of making a living, he says, we have become exemplars of "liberty under law." We have achieved a "remarkable degree of economic democracy" and "the expanding free enterprise economy means greater independence for individuals and groups." Finally, says Professor Salvadori, although poverty and other evils are relatively less serious problems in the U.S. than elsewhere, Americans are more aware of them and complaints are thus louder.

In the brief space of this introduction I cannot pay my respects, as I should like to do, to each part of this distinguished report card, nor can I give myself the pleasure of arguing a few points of interpretation. I can only point to what seems to me to be most noteworthy as a theme running through the book. This theme is that the Founding Fathers did their work with a genius unique in history, that the American people are devoted to the principles of government established at the beginning and thereafter consistently developed, and that today they still feel that this nation has a mission in the world.

All this adds up to a far more favorable verdict than would be given by a comparable group of indigenous American experts. If there is a contemporary reluctance to praise the American achievement and virtues, I fear this reluctance does not arise altogether from a sense of modesty or a fear of complacency. The question is whether, in our modern sophistication and even morbidity, some vital element of devotion to the American proposition is being lost.

President Thomas H. Hamilton of the University of Hawaii, quoting a recent syllabus for a seminar on the American tradition, observes that "the analysis of politics has turned in a direction completely alien, to all appearances, to that of the early American past. Instead of the terms *rights, equality, law, freedom*, we find *influence, power, elite, class*." These later terms do have analytical value, of course. But I would join President Hamilton in raising the question as to whether "our social sciences have become too descriptive, too reluctant to deal with values."

The writers of this volume are by no means naïve. Widely and deeply knowledgeable, they have, so far as I can see, taken note of every fault and blemish on the American scene. Yet, in the main, they have found that Americans are still characterized by an unusual degree of devotion to the values for which their country has stood. Let us hope that a similar verdict can be rendered 20 or 30 years from now—that even at the height of our achievement and in an era of radical change, this present generation will be able to pass on to its children the quality of devotion so clearly recognizable in our forefathers.

HENRY R. LUCE
Editorial Chairman, Time Inc.

The Neptune Veteran Fireman Association band from nearby Newburyport leads a Memorial Day parade down a street in Ipswich, Mass.,

followed by boys on bicycles and the American Legion color guard.

1

The Practical Idealists

by PATRICK O'DONOVAN

AS deceptively as a great, lazy fish lying for the taking in a clear pool, the United States eludes capture. It is impossible to grasp whole and entire. There is no single view, no man, no building in front of which a stranger can halt and say, "This is it!" It is contradictory and deceptive. It has no physical center. But an amateur parade, marching and laughing down the Main Street of any town, this, perhaps, comes close to summing up and expressing the nature of the place.

The parade is unlikely to be very beautiful or very heart-stirring. It will be led by high-stepping girls in semi-male costumes with all the emphasis concentrated on their tights-covered and tasseled legs. It will include unmelodious high-school bands in which boys and girls bang and tootle under tufted shakos or military caps and play so quickly that they mince along in a manner that is the reverse of military. There will be homemade floats that may be little more than advertisements for a chemical fertilizer or a supermarket. There may be politicians in open cars. There may be veterans in tiny fore-and-aft caps trying to recall their youth and look serious and responsible at the same time. There will be flags carried by youths as stiff and ungainly as toy soldiers, the Stars and Stripes carried with a religious reverence. And the pavements will be lined with men and women who recognize that this is for pleasure as well as celebration.

There are countless excuses for such parades. It may be the celebration of Independence; it may mark the recognition of the national day of Ireland, or Christopher Columbus' birthday—for the Italian-Americans. It may mark the opening of a new store or the homecoming of a local hero. (A luxury version marks the Inauguration of the President in Washington.) It is likely to be noisy. It is likely to go on too long, and its organization will lack the usual precision of American planning. But it will contain no quality of menace. It will be wonderfully innocent. Whatever its occasion, it will be a celebration, almost as repetitive as the Mass itself, of the essential, the central American myth.

Now, it is possible to tell the character of a country from its myths at least as well as from its economic statistics or its current politics. The myths may be largely true or false. But they serve to enshrine, as nothing else, a nation's view of itself. They serve to shore up the individual, to dignify the routine vulgarities of government and to put a gloss on ugly necessities. And the essential American myth is one of vernal innocence. America sees itself set apart from all the other nations by its primal innocence, by its good intentions and by its dedication, at home and abroad. It is the only nation in the world that has set itself the conscious goal of doing good. That the United States is often wrong, misinformed, self-deceiving or even perverted by some current emotion is beside the point. Under God and above all, it means well.

Americans do believe that they have something that no other people has. And in believing this particular myth of moral dedication they are probably justified. Furthermore, most of them vaguely believe that it came as the gift of a divine power, which, in

politics at least, is always left dogmatically undefined.

This myth in practical terms also means that, to Americans, America is still a young and inexperienced country. This part of the myth is dying, dying now of the patent impossibility of fitting it to the facts. It is still expressed occasionally in an almost insulting deference to the European humanities. But like all potent myths—and this one is more potent than the Glory of France or the Inherent Right of the English to Govern—it contains at its heart a colossal truth.

FOR America was born of a revolution, of a republic set against a monarchy. It was composed of men who broke oaths to assert their wishes. It used armed insurrection and occasional personal violence. But, having suffered its revolution—seen in the England of the time more as a rebellion than as a fundamental turning over of the old order—the new country set its mind to avoiding a repetition of the excesses of revolution, if possible, for all time. It was an act of reason and an act of will, and this one calculated act of creation was in fact the sweetest, the most reasonable and the most fecund act of revolution in history.

It was a revolution incited and planned by Northern merchants and intellectuals. It was conducted largely by country gentlemen of Virginia, by established magistrates, by clerks intoxicated by the 18th Century, by the solid leaders of small communities.

But what emerged was not a new and naked country struggling to find an identity and a way of life. It was an English revolution—approved of by many Englishmen at "home"—conducted by Englishmen subject to the same intellectual influences that beat on England.

In fact, the United States came into being full-grown. It was already the heir of great traditions, with as much claim to Chaucer and his peers as any Londoner. Its leaders were not raw colonials. In fact, they had among them a group of men, among the

PATRICK O'DONOVAN, born in London in 1918 of Irish parents, attended Christ Church, Oxford, from 1937 to 1939. Joining The Irish Guards soon after the outbreak of World War II, he saw extensive action as a tank officer in Europe. He went to the London *Observer* in 1946 and served as a correspondent in Israel, Greece, the Far East and the U.S. He is now a senior roving correspondent for the *Observer*. He has written extensively and provocatively on American life for both his own paper and other periodicals.

greatest of their time, not single-voiced—they even divided on some fundamentals—but a rare and marvelous coincidence of reluctant revolutionaries, of thinkers and doers that could not have been equaled in any other country of the time. If there was an act of God, then this was it, and the United States started with a spiritual capital that has not yet been spent.

These revolutionaries were uniquely practical men. Those who finally set the pattern of the new state did not believe in the perfectibility of man. They disagreed profoundly among themselves, but with pain and muddle and ferocious controversy they achieved a consensus of opinion which is still that of the United States. They believed that tyranny was the ultimate evil and was avoidable—and they included the mindless mob in their list of tyrants. They believed that real freedom, if properly established and properly protected, was possible and that under this freedom man would achieve his highest good. They believed that government should be a moral act. They believed in a permissive society—always excepting the essential checks on the innate beastliness of man. They believed that their country had no ambitions except to cultivate its own estates—which were admittedly vast enough to satisfy any imperial power. They did not believe in America so much as they believed in the possibility of a public virtue untried since the Roman republic and in the conscious dedication of the state to virtue. With "life, liberty and the pursuit of happiness" came the stern obligations and the careful limitations. All this was an afterthought to their very English rejection of England. But it was the sort of thought put into practice that England could not have achieved.

THEY clothed these ideas with a written Constitution which may be one of the supreme political works of man and which is certainly the supreme political work of any committee in history. The ideas permeated the whole society. The result, particularly when expressed with a popular or uneducated credulity, could be offensive or baffling. Nineteenth Century English writers who visited the United States found the day-to-day expression of these ideas irritating. They contrasted, in their books and articles, the manners of the Americans at the common tables of their rooming houses with their fantastic confidence and pretense to a pitying superiority. It was not just that Americans were brash and uncultivated.

They possessed a true pride, and it was this pride that visitors like Charles Dickens found intolerable. Mark Twain, particularly when abroad, singularly exemplified this pride. American ministers to the Court of St. James's found themselves unabashed in the presence of Queen Victoria, even though they alone refused court dress. A tobacco-chewing drummer in dry goods felt and expressed himself the equal of the heaped-up nobility of Europe and made it plain when he came across them. He or his fathers had crossed the Atlantic to get out of the rut of privileged society and the whole glittering edifice of kings and bishops and titled folk, of formal manners and insincerity, and, dammit, he was in a country where his son could be President and what do you think of that? It was and it still is heady stuff. And it is still working.

BEHIND the boasting and the brashness there lay the idea that this place was different, that they were unique. At least one English novelist, Anthony Trollope, recognized this fact. In a curiously unread novel, *The American Senator,* he set an American politician in among English country gentlemen. The politician is made uncultivated, loud and ignorant. He is a figure of fun tolerated by the rural apparatus of squires, vicars, gamekeepers and workers who know their place. His ideas and clumsiness make nothing but trouble for the rigidly settled and indeed beautiful community. He is humiliated in the end by that old effortless superiority. And yet, at the book's end, it is clear that he is the possessor of an idea and a purpose far higher than that of any of his opponents, hosts and tolerators.

There was, and there still is, an element of a sense of inferiority in the feeling that led to overassertion. The American might feel that the stranger was corrupt and he sturdy and self-reliant and free. But there remained the facts of European wealth and power that were not affected by American successes. There was the persistent contempt Europe so often showed America. There was the conviction—quite untrue— that the Americans' plain-minded, common-sense, village-honesty approach to foreign negotiation cost them dearly at every diplomatic contact with the outside world. And there was the poise, the confidence, the elegance and the swift speech of the strangers they knew were inferior. Only the strangers did not look or behave inferior. Today, with the experience of power and the sight of their national doorstep crowded with suppliants, the sense of inferiority has almost gone. It only remains for America generally to discover, as wholeheartedly as Europe has, the splendor of its cultural tradition.

The idea, because it was a human one and left to humans to execute, has proved imperfect. It has, however, led to the nearest approximation to democracy in the world, and this in one of the largest states of the world. And because a very real freedom went with this democracy, it imposed no single discipline, but allowed the survival of anomalies and contradictions. Such survivals are evidence anywhere of a basic freedom.

Too often in the past the sophisticated European looking in on America saw the uproarious history, the indifference to public decorum, the use of loose language in high places, the personal bargaining that accompanies politics—and dismissed it all as jejune and rather vulgar. That at least has changed. Europeans now recognize that the United States has the most subtle and complex political system in the world. A knowledge of its working is essential to anyone who would regard himself as politically educated. The most unlikely dons study U.S. history. Americana—that overworked source of European self-reassurement—has become a thing for the connoisseur, to be treated with affectionate reverence.

BUT the danger in writing of America is generalization. And the more you learn of it and the more you experience it, the harder it is to define it satisfactorily. It refuses to stay pinned to the cork. The longer you contemplate it, the more it comes to resemble some vast, mad mansion. Its ancient core at the center is elegantly planned, but around it, unplanned and unbelievably elaborate, there have been encrusted staterooms and cellars and odd towers and dark passages and rooms forever locked and functional offices and workrooms for faceless servants. Close to, it is a multilevel pile, mixing splendor and comfort and squalor. Stand back—and it is a stately, confident edifice reaching up, almost presumptuously, toward the sky.

How does one generalize about a country that is furiously democratic, whose origin lay in a conscious rejection of the European edifice of king, bishop, nobleman and subject—and which yet retains one of the few surviving, genuinely exclusive aristocracies of the world?

That this should even be thought to be so is an offensive heresy to most Americans. But in a dozen cities like St. Louis, Boston, Charleston, Baltimore, Philadelphia and even Washington, D.C., you find them flourishing, less mobile than even the French aristocracy, less showy and less tolerant than the British. They are not synonymous with "society." They tend to play a considerable role in public service, and they provide more than their share of senators and congressmen. They are not easily recognized by strangers since they share the regional accents of America. Yet there they are, an impenetrable, cultivated nucleus whose chief aim is neither wealth nor power—though they usually have both already—but the preservation of their identity: the bloodline. All over America, there are these small, camouflaged citadels of the purest snobbery.

OR again, there are the Daughters of the American Revolution. No foreigner can resist the Daughters. Profoundly snobbish in intent, qualifying for membership only by their place in the studbook, wildly reactionary, elderly, powerless and utterly innocent, they should be a pious upper-class sodality in a place like Portugal. They meet once a year, decked out in a fearful panoply of sashes and orders and hats that only need cream to be served as dessert. They pass resolutions that could be dangerous if they were effective. They tend to regard even the Bill of Rights as subversive.

They are tolerated, because they are at heart respectable and because they have acquired some of the unexpected respect Americans accord the past. The international image of America is one of organized impatience. Away with the old, the obsolete and merely picturesque! In fact, the American past is marvelously and extravagantly preserved. All over the country, exquisitely kept up or reconstructed, are the aediculae of the distant past: smithies, Presidential birthplaces, chapels and meetinghouses, blockhouses against the British or the Indians, and all looking, in their desperate, small and ground-clinging humility, remarkably alike.

This passion for the past in a country reputed to have eyes only for the future takes one extraordinary form. Many of the public rulers of the United States, not the financiers, corporation lawyers or intellectuals, but the men who create policies—the senior members of the Executive branch, the more exposed civil servants, the courtiers around the White House and the great officers of state who now serve the Presidency, the journalists who do the public thinking and agonizing—these tend to camp out in an antique enclave in Washington. It is a unique concentration of Executive and politico-intellectual power. Furthermore, if such a place existed in Europe, it would dominate all the travel posters and be damned by the impatient and the progressive as far too expensive, exclusive and pretty.

This is Georgetown. It is the exquisitely embalmed corpse of a little upriver town that was a tobacco port when America was a colony. Its vicissitudes have been odd. It served as a temporary resting place while the new city of Washington, commanded by the Revolution out of the mud, was rising. Much of it went sadly downhill, to become a Negro quarter. Then, starting with the clever young men who flocked to Washington to serve Franklin Roosevelt, it became "amusing" and then acceptable and now overwhelmingly grand. And so the public rulers, these men of undoubted power and ambition, compete at great expense for small, elegant houses of considerable inconvenience that were built for tobacco merchants, tradesmen, or the early and usually temporary inhabitants of the new city.

In Williamsburg, Virginia, they have gone further in the pursuit of preservation than any other people in the world. They have started creating, rebuilding the colonial capital on a site where little remained. They have built the British governor's palace from old plans, relined the streets with replicas of cottages, filled the gardens with contemporary herbs and put a throne for the governor in the parish church. And the result is neither meretricious nor silly, but awesome in the longing shown for the irrecoverable past.

IT is not only the Southern states that luxuriate in a past that has been given the authority of a great myth. In the North there survive small towns and villages that, with wood painted dazzling white on brick foundations, seem the physical expression, pure, Protestant and austere, of the first ideal. Their houses make a faint gesture toward England; the steepled porticoes of their churches bow toward St. Martin's-in-the-Fields. But spread, not huddled, round a common land, standing each aloof in self-disciplined independence, as beautiful

ACID ILLUSTRATION from Mrs. Frances Trollope's critical book, *Domestic Manners of the Americans* (1832), contrasts the dignity of Rome *(left)* with the debauchery of young America.

as plain things perfectly made can be, these houses and churches are another hint at the strange intellectual richness of the beginning.

And then, on top of all this, all up and down the country, beside the road, by insignificant bridges or at the edge of woods, there are signboards that proclaim the triumphant agony of the people. Here a skirmish with Indians, here a bloody battle, here a colonial mill where men struggled to shape iron, here the beginning of an almost Israelite journey across the desert. For a Britisher they make sad and compulsive reading.

So there exists both snobbery and a lust for the past that could hardly be matched in England. And that this should be so is inconsistent with the popular image of the country held alike by foreigners and citizens. It is also inconsistent with the natural working of an economy that detests all fetters, that, apparently, sees almost any attempt at discipline, even in the public good, as the onrush of Socialism. For this economy has also produced the American townscape, as incoherent as a mob in action, a bewilderment of neon signs, of great architectural styles miniaturized to suit eating places or gas stations, a fantastic, always unfinished confusion of lights and advertisements, of the new elbowing out the old, of vacant lots, of neglect and ostentation, of flags and plastic banners, of wide and broken sidewalks, of cars, assertive, dangerous and impersonal, rushing past like logs going down a river chute and, like logs again, piling up along the banks. And, as in any thicket, the unsortable details of this jungle are repeated a thousand times in a thousand places. And it all somehow has a vitality and a promise lacking in its deadly, undying European equivalents.

But such apparent inconsistencies are essential. The popular image is also, in the same limited way, true. The original idea that bore America did contain certain fastidious and aristocratic undertones. But it also implied a sort of working egalitarianism. And this egalitarianism, as the English tradition weakened, has grown to be one of the accepted principles of American life. It is sought more passionately than in Russia. It is more often broken than observed, since it appears to be, like most ideals, humanly unattainable. It is not applied to economics. But it is this reaching out toward equality that first meets Europeans at the docks and makes America seem genuinely foreign.

IT has myriad ways of expressing itself. There is the elaborate camaraderie of the politician which has reduced indiscriminate friendliness to an almost 18th Century formality, the first name (reduced where possible to a single syllable), the arm on the shoulder, the warm handclasp and the mock-humble announcement of his own name. There are waitresses being so carefully insolent to customers that the social roles are almost reversed. There are bus drivers being surly and impatient, taxi drivers didactic, telephone girls intimate, and the whole pedestrian population of New York apparently dedicated to conveying the impression that you are unwelcome and who are you anyway? All this hostility expresses the idea that "I'm at least as good as you are." And the hostility is every now and again illuminated and changed by some gratuitous and overwhelming act of private kindliness, of the most courteous acceptance of inconvenience in the service of a stranger, and you remember that you are in an alien country that pays a great deal more than lip service to its towering ideals.

It is wrong to condemn the United States for an obvious falling short of its ideals. The expression of great ideals is condemned to failure. Christianity has not made Europe a gentler place than the Orient. Christianity has certainly helped to differentiate Europe from Asia, leaving it with a radically different attitude to suffering, sin and technology. But in practical terms every Christian is a confessed failure and the validity of Christianity is not changed. The American ideal suffers from a similar strength and

weakness. The ideal is there, and the extreme American liberal who cries shame and disgrace upon almost everything American is really condemning his country for not observing his conception of the ideal. The extreme and furious Right Wing is likely to be doing just the same.

The presence of this ideal cannot be ignored; the United States would not and could not exist without it. It is the single unifying factor.

The United States has no central shrine or symbol to glorify and epitomize the ideal. There is the flag, treated with a somewhat contrived reverence; yet there are still parts of the country where people in their pursuit of their version of the American ideal prefer—or say they do—a quite different flag, the battle flag of the defeated South. The President is immersed in politics, and though the office is revered, his person is a legitimate target for almost any sort of vilification. The city of Washington itself is a many-palaced capital, but the palaces are public places. It was born of an act of will and built in a sea of mud and its leaders are at heart transients. It has a boardinghouse mentality, and it is still an object of suspicion to many Americans.

PHYSICALLY and politically, then, the United States in practice seems more disparate than any other viable state outside the frontiers of imperialism or tyranny. There are sound reasons for this. In theory it is a union of sovereign states, and to a minority the theory is very important and real indeed. It is unbelievably big. To fly to San Francisco from New York is as arduous as to fly from New York to London. It has no national press. Regionalism is regarded as part of the ancient virtue; it is regretted when it disappears. It begins to look a wonder, not that the American people had a civil war at all, but that they had only one.

For federations—if they are real—are fragile things. And in the United States each state is cluttered with all the physical apparatus of sovereignty. Each has a capitol building—usually domed—built in various degrees of ostentation or eclecticism. The United States shared with the 19th Century Roman Catholic Church a lean architectural period for its expansion.

Each has a governor, who may be urbane, a statesman of world class, or a war-horse politico who has been elevated by the squalid calculation of men who run affairs as a mechanic supervises a machine. He may also be a man who cultivates a façade of vulgarity—to demonstrate his egalitarianism—cultivating the shirt-sleeved, cigar-chewing, Bible-brandishing, damp-under-the-armpits approach as carefully as diplomats do their French accents.

Each will have its senate and house—except Nebraska, which has a single chamber—its Speaker, its own judiciary, and its police force dressed in a distinctive and occasionally theatrical uniform. Some of the legislatures dispose of budgets larger than those of European states. Some sponsor great universities. And some are Portuguese poor. But each, in law, is a state, with different laws and electoral customs.

And each of these states, boasting of its sovereignty and of its unique beauties and opportunities, each sends up two "ambassadors plenipotentiary" to the Congress in Washington. These are U.S. senators. They are compelled to represent the sovereign interests of their states in the federal legislature—whatever their private and passionate convictions on national or international questions—or else be sure of losing their high seats. It seems an impossible way in which to run a country.

It is certainly an extravagant way of running one, and America pays a high price for its system in political inefficiency. The system was consciously designed for a far smaller country to prevent the brisk and brutal efficiency of a dictatorship, to prevent even the limited effectiveness that springs from the endless delegation of powers within the British way of doing things. America is able and prepared to pay this price.

THE state system itself, with its somewhat theoretical insistence on the sovereignty of each component state, looks at first both extravagant and outmoded. The representatives and senators sent up to Washington must compete, in terms of raw politics rather than of cool planning, for the favors, the dams, highways and industries that can be provided by the federal Government. And yet, out of this hubbub a pattern emerges. From it the world's greatest economy—admittedly flawed—has emerged.

These conflicting and wordy state loyalties can grow very tedious to a stranger. But they are not nationalism, not in any new-state African sense. They represent a method of devolution in so vast a country. They further mitigate the possibility of a central, civil service absolutism. And they provide an outlet for a political emotion that will be essential as long as man is imperfect. They can be grossly exaggerated by observers. And, except in the more clinically disturbed parts of the South, all this conflicting emotion is, in the end, left subject to the insistent discipline of the common ideal.

That this impossible-seeming system should work in practice—and America works and its success cannot be jealously ascribed merely to its size and natural wealth—is the result of the power and the wisdom of the ideal. The actual interpretation of the ideal will vary a little from place to place. But it is accepted even in the South, though there its physical expression in Washington and in the federal courts is often furiously rejected. And yet the sons of those same rejectors will come forward as the best front-line soldiers of the United States in time of war.

THE interpretation again varies in the Midwest. Here there is a careful downgrading of conventional good manners, but not of hospitality. Here a basic egalitarianism is expressed often in disrespect. To a stranger, the life here can seem oddly unadorned. There is comfort but little luxury. There is culture, but it seems strained and often amateur. Here there is the extra, lingering dimension of a frontier insecurity. It is not really a frontier any more, but the frontier has left behind a sense of precarious victory that can lead to ostentation and overassertion. It is not hardship to live here. But men retain a sense of personal struggle. As a region the Midwest faces the world with a virtuous sense of superiority and resents its not being recognized. It may in fact be a rather dull place to visit, but then virtuous people are often dull. And sometimes, as in Chicago, the sense of struggle and effort breaks out in a great and rather terrible city that is one of the most exciting places in the world.

There are ill-digested anomalies like Texas, which seem not wholly to have assimilated the American ideal. This state sometimes seems, as does North Germany to Europe, unpredictable and dangerous, given to exaggerating the splendors of its own traditions and achievements. And yet it can foster—as part of that exaggeration perhaps—magnificent architecture and true scholarship. It is a place of almost conscious gratitude for the gift of life, where energy is a virtue in itself. Here, in the air, indefinable, is the expressing of a conscious delight in the privilege and achievement of being born American. It is churlish and mean to resent such an innocent delight.

There is the new phenomenon of California. This is the end of the rainbow, where the sun shines and food grows like weeds and men are accorded a unique well-being. Men who cross seas and deserts to find freedom usually dream of some earthly paradise, a happy valley, where life becomes sweet and easy. No such place exists, but California has been given this role because it is so blessed and because it is as far as you can go. This is the magnet that, like the moon to the tides, draws America slowly and inexorably toward the West. Even now, it is the most populous of all the states. And this is a new sort of civilization, built on the demand of well-being for all. In fact, like all earthly paradises, it must disappoint. It is overcrowded and ill-planned. It is also curiously discontented spiritually, given to eccentricity and extravagance, not complacent, but apparently bewildered because human complications and miseries persist.

If these seem hard strictures to lay upon the Midwest, Texas and California, the same standard of judgment would condemn as historic, unforgivable failures most of the countries of the Old World. These American regions aimed so high that their target at times seems out of human reach.

There is New England, white upon green, whose inhabitants know that they, still, are the repository of the original idea. Here are awkward, spiky towns, and fields a man can work alone. Here are hard-faced, common-sense men, as touchy as Spanish dons, hardworking, servantless, and yet with an intolerant and aristocratic outlook. Here, without any justification, the Britisher tends to feel at home. Here the old is enfolded easily into the new. Here is still the hard, impenetrable core of the United States. Its countryside is picturesque in a European manner, but these are Americans who live here, pawky and civic-minded and difficult and great.

THERE is the great megalopolis that stretches from Boston through New York and Philadelphia to Washington, D.C. Here is the vastest, richest city ever known. Here is everything the world can offer, except perhaps the luxury of unquestioning service and the beauty of mature old age. Here is industry, brutal, ugly, endlessly inventive. Here is pride and poverty and the wastage of a careless industrial

revolution—and the roots of American power.

There are the great, single-minded cities of Detroit and Pittsburgh and a dozen others where an act of will in the direction of culture sugars the pill. But here money is the *raison d'être,* and men have joined these communities, like monks a monastery, to this essential end. And where the cities have a magnificence, it is almost accidental, a by-product of the American way of getting rich.

There are great plains, cultivated by a handful of men, where the traveler stares in grateful wonder at a water tower and a huddle of blistered wooden houses. There are deserts where an incautious driver can die as surely as in the Sahara. There are snow-capped mountains, and Alph-like rivers running through impossible canyons, and gently rolling farmland that is almost bewildering in its beauty. There are monasteries, and sectarian settlements dedicated to unattainable ideals. There are sad reservations for Indians. There are ghettos for Negroes, and some of the most splendid museums in the world. There are ranch houses decorated with French Impressionists and wooden houses with wire-screened porches where the clock stopped in 1890.

BUT in the last instance the differences are subordinate, even the differences in wealth. Of course they increase the bitterness and pleasure of politics. They matter profoundly in domestic affairs and sometimes impinge on the international. But they are dwindling. In an apartment in Brooklyn and a mansion in Charleston the usually temporary occupier will eat the same breakfast food, read the same columnists and watch the same soap operas. The very differences have produced a national type that foreigners can recognize, not merely the blue-rinsed widow, the tight-suited executive or the shirttailed student. It is a type, mental and physical, black and white, that the rest of the world recognizes as easily as a Scandinavian. The differences are almost all only aspects of a whole, and the differences are only rich variations on an original theme. The whole is the fruit of the common diet, the common history and the common aspirations. Above all, all these things have been conditioned by that great potent idea, the idea of the possibility of a virtuous and happy state suggested by the Founding Fathers. Because this is believed and, in various ways, observed, it is valid. And because it is valid it works.

Shiny cars contrast with simple, brick-fronted structures along Main Street in Stroudsburg, Pa., in a scene repeated across the U.S.

Many, Varied Countries within a Single Nation

The enormous, sprawling United States is in reality many countries. Even though modern communications are diminishing the people's regional differences, the landscape remains disparate. The tidy air of rural New England bears no relationship to the hard look of the metropolis; the rolling, fertile plains are a thing apart from the majestic cruelty of the desert. All these dissimilar environments have helped to shape that elusive character, the American, as described in the foregoing chapter by Patrick O'Donovan. Mr. O'Donovan's words are used as headlines for the illustrations on the following pages.

"New England, white upon green, the repository of the original idea . . . the hard, impenetrable core of the United States. . . ."

A graceful Gothic church tops a rise in Ipswich, Mass.

Shadows slice across the lawns of Kennebunkport, Me

Spring's blossoms bring an unexpectedly gay and festive air to the spare, orderly townscape of Yarmouth, Me.

The still waters of an inlet reflect a jumble of structures in Cape Porpoise, Me.

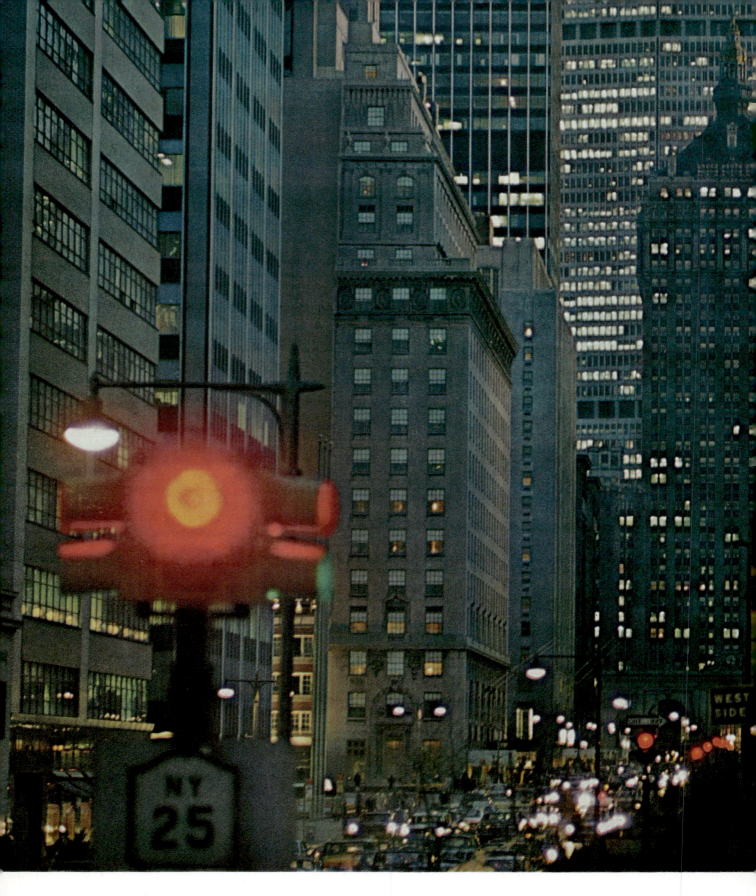

"Here is the vastest, richest city ever known . . ."

At dusk lights blink on in shiny, new office buildings along once-residential Park Avenue in New York, dotting the sides of what has become a commercial canyon.

"... *gently rolling farmland that is*
almost bewildering in its beauty ..."

*From the air the scrupulously tended perfection
of the farming country of Pennsylvania's Lancaster
County seems to roll on endlessly to the horizon.*

". . . *deserts where an incautious driver can die as surely as in the Sahara.*"

*In bleak grandeur a group of hard, steep-sided buttes rises
from the sandy, desolate landscape of Monument Valley in Arizona.*

"California . . . a new sort of civilization, built on the demand of well-being for all . . ."

Sailboats decorate the placid lagoon of Belvedere, Calif., as San Francisco's towers loom brightly across the Bay.

26

2

Reinterpreting an Elusive Past

by MARCUS CUNLIFFE

THE past matters, to every country. This is true in the most obvious sense: the sense in which "history" means everything that has happened, everything that has gone to form what we are. If men feel trapped and defeated by the past, they regard themselves as its victims. Except for Southerners, with their special heritage of thwarted hopes, Americans generally do not think in this way. If men feel sustained by the past, they regard themselves as its beneficiaries—a conviction held by most Americans.

In a slightly less obvious sense, "history" means living tradition, a set of precedents that serve as guides to conduct. One would expect this kind of history not to count much for America, whose past is a record of continuous and striven-for change. In becoming a nation the United States had in some

degree to repudiate its colonial, subservient past. Each immigrant recapitulated in miniature the national act of repudiation; he set his face toward the future. Nor did he stay put. The true American, as the French observer Michel Chevalier noted in the 1830s, "is always disposed to emigrate . . . from the place where he had but just now landed. He is devoured with a passion for locomotion. . . ." The idea of planned obsolescence existed long before the phrase was coined. Chevalier's contemporary and fellow countryman Alexis de Tocqueville was told by an American sailor that ships in the United States were built to last only a few years: their design would be out-of-date by the time they were worn out.

What could the lessons of the past usefully teach in so restless an environment? By the end of the 19th

Century the young nation of former colonies that stretched along the Atlantic seaboard was altered out of all apparent recognition. "History is bunk," cried Henry Ford, one of the great disrupters of American ways of living. By 1965 the original population of four million, predominantly of British stock, had soared to a figure of nearly 200 million, amazingly heterogeneous in make-up. A land of farms and wilderness had seen the mushrooming of factories, cities and suburbs. The small business had yielded to the giant corporation. If the symbolic American of early days was a backwoods pioneer, he was now perhaps a commuter. Buckskin or homespun was replaced by mass-produced suitings. In place of rifle and pouch he carried a newspaper and a briefcase. When George Washington became President, there were fewer men in federal employment than labored for him on his Mount Vernon plantation. A century and a half later the federal Government was prodigiously large and powerful. The young nation was isolated in fact and insular in outlook, and relied for defense upon an Army of a few thousand men and an equally tiny Navy. By the middle of the 20th Century, America's isolation was gone forever; the nation's defense budget was astronomical; its armed forces were deployed all over the globe.

Yet of course much of the past survived in the American imagination, in part because some of these changes were relatively recent and perhaps not as overwhelmingly complete as we have been taught to think. The Henry Ford who was one of the most drastic innovators in his country's history, and who expressed contempt for history, also said (in his autobiography): "It was an evil day when the village flour mill disappeared." He revived folk dancing, subsidized the publication of McGuffey's Readers (on which bygone generations of American children had been reared), assembled relics of the past (a steamboat, an old schoolhouse, the alleged birthplace of Stephen Foster) at Greenfield Village near Detroit, and in a similar venture at Sudbury, Massachusetts,

built a new section of the Boston-to-Worcester turnpike at his own expense to detour the traffic away from his idyllic reconstruction.

This is nostalgia, an emotion understandably common in America: pioneers always regret a little the passing of old ways, which their own activity has brought about. The same genial contradiction could be discerned in former Senator Barry Goldwater, a jet pilot with a love for the horse-and-buggy days of his pioneer grandfather, a man who flies the American flag outside his Arizona home but has its raising and lowering controlled by an electronic device. But something more than wistfulness is at stake when, as in the Senator's case, nostalgia serves as the basis for a Presidential campaign. There is here a very considerable involvement with the past, and one shared with millions of other Americans.

POLITICS, indeed, is one of the areas of American life on which the past lays a surprisingly heavy hand. One reason is that the American political system is built to accommodate diverse interests. Voices from the past—Southern state-rights conservatives, rural constituencies in general—may therefore exert a disproportionate influence. Another reason is that voters and politicians alike are responsive to—or are believed to respond to—national myths that may be of quite ancient ancestry—including the presumed preference for candidates from rural or small-town America. A more fundamental reason is that America is still living under a Constitution devised in 1787—the oldest of such surviving documents in the entire world. Though some of its provisions, including the Electoral College, now have little relevance, the Constitution is still very much an instrument of government. Associated with it is that venerable body, the Supreme Court, for which the precedents of the past are constant touchstones. No one was surprised when in a 1964 decision concerning civil rights the Court reached back as far as 1824 for a rule (*Gibbons* v. *Ogden*) of the great Chief

MARCUS CUNLIFFE, who was born in Lancashire, England, in 1922 and attended Oriel College, Oxford, is a leading British authority on U.S. history and culture. Formerly Professor of American History and Institutions at the University of Manchester (England), he became Professor of American Studies at England's new University of Sussex in 1965. The author of *George Washington: Man and Monument* and *The Literature of the United States*, he has also studied and taught at Harvard, Yale and Stanford.

Justice John Marshall. On the other side, Governor Orval Faubus in 1957 could draw upon a body of state-rights doctrine going as far back as Thomas Jefferson in support of segregation in Arkansas. Ancient creeds of this nature are not kept alive solely by eccentrics or extremists. The old Jeffersonian slogan, "That government is best which governs least," had surely more than an antiquarian appeal for a President as moderate as General Eisenhower.

THERE is a third, related sense in which history affects and reflects our attitudes: "history" as the record of the past, "history" as what historians have said about the past. One of America's foremost historians, Frederick Jackson Turner, called this "subjective history," i.e., theory, our conception of events, as opposed to "objective history," i.e., facts, the events themselves. Subjective history flourishes in all countries; we may doubt whether, despite Turner, there is any other kind. But it certainly flourishes in the United States. American historians, for all their cool professionalism, still engage in fierce controversy over practically every major issue in the nation's past. They still take sides and still find fresh evidence bearing on, say, the extension of suffrage in the late 18th Century, or the Bank War of the 1830s, or the origins of the Civil War, or the effects of Reconstruction, or whether it would not be more accurate as well as politer to refer to the Robber Barons of the late 19th Century as Industrial Statesmen—to mention only zones of dispute that lie before the beginning of our own controversial century. The enduring nature of such disputes is a testimony to the resonance of American history, as well as to the vigor of American historiography (writing about history). The disputes have run on through the various emphases of successive generations of scholars: through the grand digressions on American virtue of George Bancroft's day and the post-1865 moralisms of Hermann von Holst; through the geographic and economic preoccupations of Turner and Charles A. Beard, in their different ways; through the radical-reformist scholarship of the first third of this century; and down to the revised revisions of the present day.

Or the point could be stated otherwise. Happy countries, we are told, have no history. Is the truth that America has been an unhappy or at any rate a complicated country? If we seek to make sense of the shifting mass of fact and theory, one feature might seem to stand out: the persistence of conflict in American history, indeed of a whole range of polarized oppositions. In part, no doubt, they are consequences of a federal form of government, built upon compromise. Even peaceful little Switzerland, another federally organized nation, does not run without friction. We would expect to see more in a huge and expanding country like the United States: friction, for example, between legislature and executive, between the federal Government and the states, between one region and another. In part, also, these dualisms have represented rival views of the desired future shape of the country. Where so much might turn upon a single decision, no wonder the discussion is likely to be heated.

SEVERAL of the chief dualisms have been polarized dramatically around the most famous antithesis of American historiography: Thomas Jefferson, the Virginian Secretary of State in Washington's first Administration, and Treasury Secretary Alexander Hamilton of New York. Jefferson represents the agrarian side of America, Hamilton the urban and commercial. Jefferson speaks for localism and state rights, Hamilton for centralized government. Jefferson typifies the movement toward democracy, Hamilton a preference for what in the American context (though hardly in the European) could be described as aristocracy. Jefferson stands for the South, Hamilton for the North. By implication Jefferson is the champion of the back country, the West; Hamilton of the Atlantic seaboard towns, the East. Here then are sketched out the main polarities of traditional American historiography:

    Jefferson vs. Hamilton
    Country vs. Town
    Agriculture vs. Industry
    States Rights vs. Centralization
    Democracy vs. Aristocracy
    South vs. North
    West vs. East

We may note, too, that Jefferson has been a patron saint of the Democratic Party and that Hamilton would appear qualified for the same role in relation to the Republicans. In politics the Jeffersonian lineage, or at least some of its elements, can be traced through Andrew Jackson, William Jennings Bryan, Woodrow Wilson, Franklin D. Roosevelt, Harry S.

Truman and John F. Kennedy, and thus down to Lyndon B. Johnson. The Hamiltonian-Federalist line would seem to have been perpetuated by Whigs like Daniel Webster, by the extended run of post-1865 Republican Administrations and in some of the Republicanism of the 20th Century, particularly that of Theodore Roosevelt, who was as scornful of Jefferson as he was respectful of Hamilton. It would look as though American politics exhibit an ancient and fairly basic cleavage, with the Democrats tending to be the party of the Have-Nots and the Republicans to be the party of the Haves. True, the pattern is not ideally neat. In the 20th Century the Democrats have borrowed the centralizing aspects of Hamiltonianism and (with the exception of their Southern wing) have yielded to the Republicans corresponding portions of Jeffersonian localism. But the fundamental division, of ends if not of means, could be argued to have remained the same.

Beyond the political alignments are other contests that provide guidelines for American historiography. Consider economic issues. To Charles A. Beard, writing in 1913, the framing of the Constitution of 1787 and the debates over ratification were explainable as a tussle between competing economic interests. More or less the same division, in this view, accounted for the Bank War of Jackson's era. Economic issues naturally took on a sectional character. Southern proslavery arguments were at least in some degree an economic protest at the subservience of the cotton economy to the manufacturing and money centers of the North. A comparable resentment generated protest movements in the West against the selfish domination of North-East capital. Pleading the cause of the lowly people of the West, the poet Vachel Lindsay wrote:

> . . . *all these in their helpless days*
> *By the dour East oppressed,*
> *Mean paternalism*
> *Making their mistakes for them,*
> *Crucifying half the West,*
> *Till the whole Atlantic coast*
> *Seemed a giant spider's nest.*

Economic resentment and sectional feeling dominated the unsuccessful Presidential campaigns of William Jennings Bryan, who thundered that the Eastern bankers, who controlled the nation's capital, were crucifying the West on a "Cross of Gold."

Earlier, Henry George in his widely read *Progress and Poverty* (1879) had divided America between the "House of Have" and the "House of Want."

It was in these groupings that Frederick Jackson Turner, the Middle Westerner from Portage, Wisconsin, thought he discerned the key to American history. In his head also was an awareness of the biggest dualism of all: that between the United States and Europe, the New World and the Old. Was the United States simply an outgrowth of Europe, explainable in European terms and possibly doomed to a derivative, second-rate destiny? Were the older areas of settlement, with their mansions for the rich and tenements for the poor, ceasing to be truly American? What *was* truly American? For Turner the unique American factor was the "ever retreating frontier" of free land. More precisely it was the interaction, again and again, of wilderness and civilization at the edge of settlement. The process was manifold, continuous and deeply significant for the American character. Each struggling frontier community was forced back close to primitivism. Men had to improvise ways of life and ways of thought. Geography was their chief instructor. The frontier was both a profound and a practical school of democracy. It transformed Europeans into Americans and made Americans the more American. American democracy was a product of the frontier, not a rubric shipped over from England, still less a mystic inheritance from ancient Germany (as Turner's historian-contemporaries, several of whom had actually been trained in Germany, seemed disposed to believe).

THE Frontier Thesis, once formulated, appeared —like other alluring generalizations—to be not a theory but a plain description of reality. It put into words what many people, especially those west of the Appalachians, thought they had always thought. Indeed, the ground had been prepared. "Westward the course of empire takes its way": the prophetic line from Bishop Berkeley's 18th Century poem was a favorite with Americans. George Bancroft adapted it for the cover of his famous history of the young nation, the first volume of which appeared in 1834. Tocqueville's *Democracy in America*, published shortly after Bancroft's volume, contains an awed reference to the inexorable process of Western settlement, marching onward across the continent at an average speed of 17 miles *per annum*. It

DEFINING THE UNIQUE CHARACTER OF A LARGE AND COMPLEX YOUNG NATION

ALEXIS DE TOCQUEVILLE   JAMES BRYCE   FREDERICK JACKSON TURNER   VERNON LOUIS PARRINGTON

INFLUENTIAL HISTORIANS who tried to capture the nature of America are shown above. Tocqueville, an uncannily perceptive Frenchman, analyzed the U.S. in *Democracy in America* (1835). Bryce, who became British Ambassador to the U.S., published *The American Commonwealth* in 1888. Turner, an American professor, wrote his essay on the frontier in American history in 1893. In 1927 Parrington, another American, published the first two volumes of *Main Currents in American Thought*.

was commonly recognized that the farther west you went the more "American" things became. "The new States of the West," Tocqueville wrote, ". . . stand in the same relation to the older States of the Union as these last stand to Europe."

The importance of Turner was that his quietly lucid pages embraced and improved on all such prior notions. Within a decade or so his was widely accepted as not merely *an* explanation but *the* explanation of American development. The admiring Woodrow Wilson, himself a historian, would have liked to bring Turner east to Princeton. Eventually, in 1910, Turner accepted the tributes of Eastern scholars and came as a professor to Harvard. His theory had conquered. It gratified the pride of Americans of every section. In early essays Turner had said that American history was "at bottom the study of European germs developing in an American environment." But clearly it was the differences, not the similarities, that counted most. The conclusion was especially gratifying to the Westerner, who had felt with some reason that the East condescended to him. Now, properly studied, his nation's past appeared as a departure, in every sense, from the East.

Though Turner was a dispassionate man his writings reflect much of the radical temper of the Populist and Progressive movements. This temper was more marked in another of the works that have deeply influenced the nation's self-analysis: Vernon L. Parrington's *Main Currents in American Thought*. Parrington began to prepare his book in 1913, although it was not published until the late 1920s. He wrote as a Jeffersonian and as a Turnerian. He laid out the dualisms of American development with the

persuasive charm of a brilliant advocate. His heroes were men of a libertarian, "Western" stamp, his villains fatally tainted with antidemocratic, "Eastern" opinions. East and West clashed economically as well as intellectually; after the Civil War they were "rival imperialisms." As Parrington saw it, their antagonism replaced the previous principal polarity of North versus South. He was enough of a Jeffersonian to regret some of the results of the Civil War.

"The old philosophies," he wrote, "were swept out on the rubbish heap—Jefferson and Lincoln with Calhoun and [Confederate Vice President] Stephens—and Hamilton and Marshall came into their own again. The lost cause carried down to defeat much more than slavery, it carried down the old ideal of decentralized democracies, of individual liberty. . . ."

Historians of the generation before his would not have agreed. To Hermann von Holst the North-South polarity was the story of genuine Americanism contending with wicked heresy, of wholesome endeavor undermined by a conspiratorial "slaveocracy." But whichever view seems more plausible, there can be no argument that much of American history could be written around the rival conceptions embodied in the clash of North and South. Here is a great, protracted conflict. The Civil War decided that the Confederacy should not break away from the Union. In this respect it may have blurred our picture. Who can say for sure that the South was not a separate nation, as it claimed to be, by 1860? The Union *did* shatter in the 1860s, even if it was glued together again. Conflict *is* part of the American frame of reference, and the study of the major polarities is a method of organizing and understanding the American past.

Yet the dualities are not the whole story. To appreciate why the United States has held together and prospered, we need to examine the unities, the cohesive as against the divisive factors, for it is the unities, and the constant search for them, that illustrate the motive force. Turner's critics believe that he underestimated the colonial and European inheritance of the United States. The Thirteen Colonies gained a solid experience in self-government. Contrasting their situation with that of the French colonies in Canada to the north, the historian Francis Parkman saw a decisive superiority. The French were ruled from home, autocratically and corruptly. Catholicism produced some heroic missionary-explorers, but did not foster the bustling independence of Protestant societies. The French fur-trapping empire, impressive on maps, was scattered and vulnerable; the British settlements were relatively compact and dense. Class distinctions in the Thirteen Colonies were less oppressive; the upper ranks were largely composed of native Americans, not of European officeholders on temporary assignments; a majority were ready to support and dignify the Revolution when it came. Unlike the "offensive" French Revolution (in the words of the Prussian scholar Friedrich von Gentz), the American one was "defensive." Content with modest goals, it achieved a successful transfer of authority. Leadership passed harmoniously from George III to George Washington and thence in orderly succession to John Adams, Thomas Jefferson and so on; whereas in France the bloody turmoil of the Terror led to Napoleon.

IN America, gradually but smoothly, the latent libertarianism of colonial times had evolved into full democracy, with further astonishing results. Democracy, Tocqueville discovered, "produces . . . a restless activity, a superabundant force and an energy which is inseparable from it, and which may . . . produce wonders." Remoteness from Europe was a distinct benefit, as the historian Samuel Flagg Bemis has pointed out. Europe's distresses were America's advantages—in distracting the British during the Revolution and the War of 1812, in enabling the young United States to secure the Louisiana Purchase from France at a bargain rate in 1803, and on subsequent occasions. On the other hand, economic

ties remained close. European and especially British capital and manufactures helped to speed the process of Western settlement. European emigration augmented the American labor supply. America flourished along with the rest of the transatlantic economy. Technological innovation—the steamboat and the railroad, the cotton gin and the McCormick reaper, the sewing machine and the lathe—quickened the pace. The continent proved to be rich in natural resources, and these were exploited with a will. All the graphs ran upward. A lucky people, the envious conceded. A chosen people, the Americans claimed.

THIS confidence in the American mission is nowhere better expressed than in the works of the mid-19th Century historians Bancroft, William Hickling Prescott and John L. Motley. Their attitude is summed up in the title of a pamphlet published by Motley in 1869: "Democracy, the Climax of Political Progress, and the Destiny of Advanced Races." They believed that history was providential. It was the story of liberty, and America was in the van. Inferior races and creeds yielded, as they must, to the superior. The white man was stronger—militarily, intellectually, morally—than the colored. The Northern (or Anglo-Saxon or Teutonic) peoples were stronger than the Southern (Latin, Mediterranean, Celtic). Protestantism was stronger than Catholicism. Democracy was stronger than any other form of government. The United States was a white, Anglo-Saxon, Protestant democracy and therefore represented the highest stage in universal history. The embattled farmers at Lexington in 1775, Bancroft assured his readers, "fulfilled their duty not from an accidental impulse of the moment. . . . The light that led them on was combined of rays from the whole history of the race. . . ."

In such language we perceive the cumulative driving force of American pride, with its amalgam of religious, democratic and acquisitive energy and its sublime confidence in what Emerson called the "unsearched might of man." These enthusiasms were the cement of the Union. American patriotism was spontaneous and strong; if it had not been, the Union effort in the Civil War would have collapsed. Native Americans and immigrants (including an ever-larger proportion who were not Anglo-Saxons and not Protestants) both subscribed to the American creed with an almost religious fervor. The items of their faith were enumerated thus by the spread-eagle orator George Francis Train in 1858: "Young America considers the Declaration of Independence, the Constitution, Washington's farewell address, Yankee Doodle, and the Bible, divine institutions. Life, liberty, and happiness, are the words in his Book of Life." America was on God's side and God was on America's.

THE creed had its inhibitions. Though it was genial and hospitable, public opinion fixed the limits of tolerance in some ways more narrowly than was the case in Europe. The norm may have been middle-class, as some European commentators said. It certainly did not run to extravagances, in conduct or in thought. Then as now, the average American was notoriously indifferent, if not actively hostile, to abstract reasoning. The isms and ideologies of Europe made no deep impression. Daniel Boorstin remarks that the United States has produced no major work of political theory for the happy reason that it has not needed to. The American contribution to political discourse has been confined to vocabulary: words like gerrymander, logrolling, caucus and pork barrel, all coined to describe politics as a bargaining, horse-trading activity—a practical and slightly seamy business, not a scholastic disputation. The American contribution to political organization has been more substantial, but again a practical rather than a theoretical affair.

To the Scottish observer James Bryce (*The American Commonwealth*, 1888) the main American political parties were like two bottles bearing different labels but with the same contents. Perhaps the key to American history, to use terms that are much bandied about nowadays, is *consensus*, as contrasted with *ideology*. (Both words are inexact. Broadly, *consensus* stands for the search for agreement, based on the belief that agreement is never very far away in the American context; *ideology* refers to an abstract, doctrinaire theory, often with radical or revolutionary implications, and therefore un-American in its very nature.) Looked at in this way unionism is a more vital element than sectionalism; the essential homogeneity of the United States may be more significant than its apparent heterogeneity. Some of the conflicts that seemed so savage may bear a milder interpretation. Beard's theory of economic cleavages over the Constitution has been riddled in the past few years. Historians are no longer so sure that Jefferson and Hamilton represented diametrically opposed tendencies. Jefferson knew that America must cease to be wholly agricultural; Hamilton realized that it had never been and could never be an aristocracy—or a plutocracy. The neat genealogy of party history begins to look less simple on closer inspection. Were the Whigs really in direct descent from the Federalists? In any case, was there any vast difference between Whigs and Democrats? Why was Abraham Lincoln a Whig?

We are forced by recent historiography to ask whether the Bank War of the 1830s or the perpetual battles in Congress over the tariff, land sales and the like testify to any deep-seated division on questions of principle. In *The Liberal Tradition in America* (1955) Louis Hartz suggests that these battles had more shadow than substance. Joseph G. Baldwin, a man who had been involved in some of them, could nevertheless view them coolly. Writing of the struggles between Andrew Jackson and Henry Clay, he said that "while the principles which have divided parties are doubtless important, it is simply ridiculous to attribute to them . . . the degree of importance attached to them by partisans. The country could have gone on under either scheme, and the difference in its condition would scarcely have been noticed."

CONSIDERATIONS of this sort have led some historians to query whether the North-South conflict was passionate and "inevitable" enough to lead to war. They have blamed the small group of abolitionists in the North and of "fire-eaters" in the South for creating a heated atmosphere in which the search for acceptable compromise failed. They have cited the "Brothers' War," the "Irrepressible Conflict," as a dreadful example of what happened when consensus was abandoned. The celebrated American Way of Life could be taken as a free translation of *modus vivendi*, that Latin tag so often appealed to by mediators. *Modus vivendi:* a way of living, a method of living together.

Other temporary fits of American extremism, happily less serious in outcome, have been held to reinforce the moral. There was the brief crusading zeal that accompanied America's entry into World War I. What followed except disillusion? There was Prohibition, that experiment "noble in motive" (as

Herbert Hoover styled it) to turn the United States into a dry nation. A cynical farce ensued. Or there were the naïvetés of Left-Wing commitment during the 1930s: high hopes, and still more disillusionment. The real lesson of the Depression, American historians might now say, was that in 1933 Germany confided its leadership to a ranting ideologue, Hitler, while America put its trust in F.D.R., a cheerful, pragmatic patrician who would not have recognized an ideology if he had met one. Indeed, what a span of American pragmatism is typified in the reaction of the Whig politician Thurlow Weed when invited to attend a lecture by a reformer: "Being tolerably well satisfied with things as they are, we remained, enjoying our segar and newspaper, in the Barber's Room." Or in these phrases from a speech by Lyndon Johnson: "It is one of the great tasks of political leadership to make our people aware that they share a fundamental unity of interest, purpose and belief. I intend to try and achieve a broad national consensus which can . . . liberate the energies of the nation for the work of the future."

DUALITIES or unities? Frontier or seaboard? Redskin or paleface? The range of choice reminds us again of Turner's "subjective history." There are no final answers. He himself has been vigorously criticized as one who mistook metaphor for hypothesis. Europe *or* America, consensus *or* ideology? One need not feel obliged to choose one or the other. In the present climate of opinion, consensus explanations are more in fashion than the other sort.

The Harvard historian Arthur M. Schlesinger Sr. once maintained that there is yet another pattern to American history—a cyclical movement in which periods of conservatism alternate regularly with radicalism. If so, the recent conservative phase with its revulsion from ideology may have induced historians to read the same mood into various episodes of the past, with greater or less justification.

Another recent tendency should be noted. Now that America is an established and even an old nation, scholars such as Reinhold Niebuhr have become concerned with the shortcomings of traditional American thought. They believe that the United States was more lucky than chosen and ought to understand that the luck may be running out. As for the past, they would have Americans grasp that the country was never as exceptional as its citizens liked to think. Economically, spiritually, Americans belonged to a larger context. The frontier influence was not negligible, nor was that of Europe. The abundance of American life wrought a sea change; yet something vital *was* carried over in the *Mayflower* with the first colonists.

WE may agree. And we may feel that both consensus and ideology are to be taken into account in interpreting the American past. Man does not live by bread alone, nor by slogans, but by both. Belief in America was itself a form of ideology. It gave Americans a certain largeness of utterance that was very striking, and sometimes irritating, to foreign observers. True, many of them seemed to foreigners to talk mainly of the Almighty Dollar. "The chief business of America is business," said Calvin Coolidge. Yet individual success was equated with national well-being. "The chief ideal of the American," Coolidge cryptically added, "is idealism." Vernon Parrington's scheme of things has lost favor with American academics. They find his polarities inadequate when no proper room can be found for Americans of the stature of Edgar Allan Poe and Henry James. Yesterday's categories are today's encumbrances. But it would be unwise to reject them out of hand. For instance, are consensus and ideology in fact mutually exclusive notions? The very stress laid upon consensus indicates that it may often have been an ideal rather than an actuality. Americans have become expert in the techniques of consensus because they had to in a country so loose in structure and diverse in opinion. Unremitting effort has been required ever since the Founding Fathers. Not all problems have been political. Aspirations exact a price: individualism has threatened to become selfishness (as Turner explained); democracy may invite uniformity and mediocrity; social mobility carries the danger of rootlessness. These phenomena were well known a century and more ago. Amid fantastic change much has remained: history matters. Parts of the ideology of Americanism may now be inert or seem irrelevant. But other parts still stir the nation's conscience, as they did for Jefferson and John Adams, Lincoln and Stephen Douglas, Theodore Roosevelt and Woodrow Wilson. On the lips of Negro students the words of the Declaration of Independence or "My Country, 'Tis of Thee" lose their banality and sting again.

Members of a group called The Civil War Round Table inspect a cannon at Sayler's Creek in Virginia, site of a Union victory.

Appreciating the Past in an Era of Swift Change

The bulldozer and wrecker's ball often seem about to obliterate all vestiges of America's past. In New York City, for example, only a few buildings remain from the "classic" era of native architecture (1750-1850). All the others have been razed as the city has gone through successive periods of change.

Despite this restless drive to tear down and build anew, Americans do love the remnants of their past and strive through them to comprehend their history. A few old houses, some famous battlefields, isolated reminders of the Old West—these are prized and preserved with an almost religious veneration.

REAL RUINS AND FAKE FIGHTS draw tourists to the West to see vestiges of Indian cultures and the white man's conquest

INTREPID TOURISTS climb a ladder *(left)* in Colorado's Mesa Verde National Park to view a cliff dwelling abandoned long ago by Pueblo Indians. Mesa Verde is the most popular of such Indian sites.

AN INTENT AUDIENCE hears a Mesa Verde Park ranger lecture on the dwellings *(right)*. The finest structures at Mesa Verde were built in the 13th Century, but the Indians had deserted the colony by 1300.

MOCK GUNSLINGERS fight a staged battle *(above)* twice a day for tourists in Abilene, Kans., formerly one of the wildest towns in the West. Old buildings, such as a bar and a hotel, have been rebuilt.

A DESPERADO'S COFFIN gives gawking tourists a grisly subject for photographs after the faked fight shown above. The gunman, played by a high-school student, led a mock raid on the town bank.

39

A SPRAWLING TRACT of new and almost identical houses, begun in 1962, stretches out across some rocky hills in southern California. The area's developers predict that it will include 35,000 homes by 1970. Many such faceless housing projects have sprung up since World War II.

A CHANGING CITY, Baltimore builds an urban renewal project in the middle of its downtown area. To make way for the project, 22 acres of the city's buildings were razed, but Baltimore enlisted the services of some of the nation's leading architects to work on the new structures.

A DESERTED SHACK, once a miner's home, is now only a shell in the forlorn town of Tomboy in the San Juan Mountains of southern Colorado.

TUMBLE-DOWN BUILDINGS are all that is left of once busy Tomboy. The town was abandoned in 1926 when its last gold mine ran out of ore.

42

GHOST TOWNS, *weird relics of another era, crumble and decay in the baking Colorado sun*

THE EMPTY MAIN STREET of Crested Butte, Colo. *(left),* is kept in repair by the town's few remaining inhabitants, who provide lodging for skiers. Strikes of gold, silver, lead, zinc and coal attracted 5,000 people to the area in the 19th Century. The last important mine closed in 1952.

FALLEN ON HARD TIMES, the James G. Blaine house in Washington, D.C., a prime example of ornate mid-Victorian architecture, has had its ground floor invaded by a supermarket.

CAREFULLY MAINTAINED, an old mansion called "San Francisco" *(right)*, built in 1850, stands on its Louisiana plantation. The house, though open to the public, is seldom visited.

CHERISHED TOWN HOUSES are preserved by city dwellers in Boston and San Francisco, and in other U.S. cities, for their beauty, comfort and links with the past

MANY-HUED BUILDINGS brighten San Francisco's Webster Street *(right)*, where the well-to-do have been restoring many late-Victorian houses. In some, lavish interior restoration has cost up to $40,000, and property values have almost doubled.

DIGNIFIED BRICK HOMES with black shutters surround Boston's Louisburg Square *(below)*. The square's houses were built by the Boston mercantile aristocracy. Former residents include the authors Louisa May Alcott and William Dean Howells.

3

The Enduring Flexibility of a Political System

by ALAIN CLÉMENT

THE most remarkable characteristic of the American political system is not its parliamentary and governmental machinery—noteworthy enough though that is—but the faith and fervor that this machinery inspires in the American people. However defective the institutions of a country may be, they will always have defenders; indeed, nations can function only if their institutions command at least a degree of popular assent. There is nothing exceptional about the attachment of modern citizens to a public order inherited from the past. What is exceptional, when one considers the American phenomenon in its living reality, is the almost religious trust that this order commands from Americans.

The explicit, spontaneous and exuberant character of this faith is manifested constantly. Millions of

American children salute the Stars and Stripes each morning at the start of the school day. References to the "Founding Fathers" and to the Constitution abound in contemporary advertisements and periodicals. On weekends and holidays hosts of tourists crowd into shrines like the Lincoln and Jefferson memorials in Washington. These manifestations of American faith contrast with the rather detached attitude of other nations, such as Britain, where tradition has always been taken for granted, and where it is only rarely the object of overt devotion and organized pomp—not to mention the inveterate skepticism of Latin and Latinized peoples toward their political institutions.

Within the Anglo-Saxon circle, Americans are not as a general rule better citizens than Englishmen or

49

Canadians. Yet even the most apathetic or under-privileged among them do not imagine that they could live under a different system—even though they may violate their own laws or suffer cruelly under them. Not even the Civil War was an attack on the American system; the South modeled its Constitution on that of the Union. It was secession, not heresy, that the South had in mind.

Fundamentally, the American system does not appear to Americans to be a mere triumph of human ingenuity in the face of great troubles and difficulties. It is more than a success, more even than a miracle; it is, to paraphrase Lincoln, the achievement of a superior destiny placed by the Almighty into the hands of his "almost chosen people" to spread "a great promise to all the people of the world in all time to come." One might almost say that the vocation of the American people is to go from one Promised Land to another, not only to move out of the Original Paradise of the Founding Fathers but to proceed toward the Eternal Paradise of mankind, gathered under a third Biblical Testament.

This feeling of American predestination and of self-wonder, served by unchanging rites and rhetoric, has astonished even the most sympathetic observers of the American republic, from Alexis de Tocqueville to Sir Denis Brogan. The certainty that American institutions are the best in the world—even when some of their defects are acknowledged—expresses itself in an "American Creed" and prolongs itself in an "American Dream."

This enthusiasm long was shared by Europe, particularly in the mid-19th Century, when liberal thought was being stifled on the Continent. Seen from the shores of Ireland, from the universities of Germany or from the czarist ghettos, America appeared to be the Promised Land. The Old World projected its unfulfilled dreams toward the New. It looked upon it as the land of unlimited hope and unrestricted initiative. The romanticized concept of the open American frontier still exercises a magnetic attraction on foreign imagination; its latest manifestation is the universal popularity of Westerns and other projections of American folklore as viewed on the screens of the whole world. This fascination reflects the fact that both Europeans and Americans thought new dimensions and broadened horizons had been introduced by the American experiment.

YET over the years Americans and Europeans have diverged in their thinking about the U.S. system. In the American mind the system remains a unified one, with institutions, economics, revered documents and symbols integral parts of the whole, much as medieval Europe was a cohesive and integrated system. Masters and serfs alike were parts of a larger whole, with a philosophical-political-religious base that justified and gave meaning to the entire structure. In the 1920s European observers introduced a distinction between American politics, which they judged rough, sterile and somehow static, and the American economic system. To American observers they thus separated the inseparable—for the average American, happy or not with his lot, feels himself framed in a totally integrated context where legend and history, realities and myths, and political and economic institutions are inextricably intermixed.

This change in the European point of view has been summarized by the British observer Max Beloff: "What impresses Europeans and others is the seeming efficiency of the American economic system, its apparent capacity to produce ever higher standards of living for the masses; while they tend to regard American political institutions as old-fashioned and even perhaps inadequate. But Americans not only accept the continued validity of their political practices, but even ascribe much of their economic success directly to them." A big corporation will not hesitate, for instance, to glorify this enchanted circle where each epoch, each family, each individual occupies a specified place that has its justification in the radiant message handed down by

ALAIN CLÉMENT, who is U.S. correspondent for the Paris newspaper *Le Monde*, is considered one of the most thoughtful and discerning foreign commentators on the American political scene. Born in Douai, France, in 1925, he joined *Le Monde* in 1948 after completing graduate studies at the Sorbonne. From 1948 until 1962 he was his paper's correspondent in Germany. Now a resident of Washington, he has become noted for his dispassionate, learned discussions of U.S. Government events and personalities.

the Founding Fathers. "The function of government," reads an advertisement extolling the qualities of trucks and heavy equipment, "was to keep everyone free—the inventors, the financial backers and those who chose to buy the product. The result was a new civilization, growing because men were free to strive and risk."

The political allusion may be clear to every reader, but it is not just propaganda, as might be the case elsewhere. References to the sacred origins of the Republic are constant in the American system, just as references to the holy fathers and thinkers of the early Church were constant in the medieval system. Some American commentators spend their lives assessing domestic political events in the light of the nation's "fundamentals." Many of these people are conservatives, but their liberal opponents do the same thing, as do ordinary citizens.

What escapes the scope of the American vision, or rather what remains in the shade, is the price this civilization has paid and the controversies it has raised. To the familiar phrase "free to strive and risk" might be added the words "as well as to fail and starve." Yet Americans do not regularly add those words. Ready as their writers are to dramatize conflicts, inequalities and past suffering—witness the plethora of books about the Civil War—they often gloss over or romanticize the ordeals through which the American community passed. This is hardly surprising, considering the American belief that American history is a series of connected episodes leading to the final glory prophesied in the Promise given to their community at its birth. The unspeakable misfortunes suffered by millions in pursuit of happiness on American territory are thought of as regrettable yet reparable accidents instead of crimes condemning an entire society, as such crimes were regarded in the 19th Century Europe that had abandoned its belief in an all-encompassing politico-economic system.

IN the U.S. the extremely brutal social and political clashes of the 19th Century shook the institutional framework, but never aimed at destroying it. In Europe, thrones were swept away, frameworks were torn down. No such development took place in America, and no such goals were formulated because the crises the American people had to surmount did not involve the principle of legitimacy, of who had the right to rule. In the United States

legitimacy was and is impersonal and abstract, and was therefore impossible to grasp and topple over, whereas in Europe legitimacy was linked to specific monarchs and dynasties. Still, a result opposite to that which actually took place in the United States might have been expected, for what restraint could an abstract form of legitimacy exert, based as it was on antiquated texts and on outmoded institutions?

RAISING this question, however, only serves to underline that it is totally irrelevant in the American context. For an American the Constitution is not the product but the source of legitimacy. It requires no justification. What derives from it is legitimate, not merely legal, and therein resides its uniqueness. The Constitution is not just an historical document doomed to obsolescence, nor the text of a "social contract" subject to repeal, but the manifestation of a Revelation, at the same time the Tables of the Law and the Ark of the Covenant, the final justification of the all-encompassing system.

One further remark would be in order here. The sacred character of the Constitution and the cult it inspires relate to something else. Once allegiance is sworn to this cornerstone of the American structure, the field is left open to competition and friction. Because of its laconic and oracular style, the Constitution lends itself to various interpretations. The Supreme Court, the highest authority in the matter of its interpretation, is not bound by precedent; it may revise and reverse its own rulings, not unscrupulously, of course, but in a spirit of independence that renders the Court's decisions as unpredictable as the unfathomable aims it discerns in the Constitution. The various "branches" of government—legislative, executive and judicial—and the indeterminate zones between form a forest hard to penetrate and differ greatly from the august trinity they are supposed to be. The parties, rival interests and opinions, and the various levels of authority are in a perpetual flux of opposition and alliance.

Their interaction amounts to a game, in the ancient and majestic sense of the word, as evidenced by the outcry that goes up whenever it is suggested that the Supreme Court be invited to give a preliminary opinion on some bill still under discussion. It is as if the umpire were asked at the beginning of a game to designate the winning side on the basis of objective criteria. The public would have been deprived of the show. The "glorious uncertainty" of the confrontation would have been dispelled. The sporting element in American political life is as deep-rooted as the ceremonial that surrounds and dignifies it. As with ancient Greece, the stadium and the altars are located in the same precinct.

While it is relatively easy to describe the legal structure of the American system or to trace its history—whole libraries have been devoted to one subject or the other—it is far more difficult to assess the system because of this continuing interaction of parties, interests, opinions and authorities, all on the field of play at once.

To understand the system it is perhaps necessary to start from the beginning and ask oneself the reasons why the American Constitution has lasted so long. As we may recall, this now-revered document was not immediately accepted by the American people, and an active campaign and exceptional procedures were required to ensure its ratification in 1788. Despite the seal of serene respectability imparted to the young American republic by the charisma of George Washington's Presidency, the new nation was subjected to internal tensions and pressures that strained its brand-new institutions. To survive these first economic and social ordeals, which resulted from a national development too rapid not to be untroubled, the new institutions had not only to function well; they had to be imbued with a spirit somehow adapted to the needs of American expansion.

THE process was to take years, but the American Constitution was to prove more than an expedient or a talisman. It transmitted to, and incorporated into, the American nation a fundamental scheme, a general pattern that provided for the development of the political and social organization of the country. The penetration in depth of this scheme in the American fabric over the following generations is extremely remarkable, considering that the Founding Fathers had not particularly distinguished themselves by the gift of prevision during their lengthy deliberations in Independence Hall in Philadelphia in the summer of 1787. They did not, so to speak, dispatch a Lewis and Clark Expedition to reconnoiter the legal ground for a possible extension of their work. They confined themselves to the solution of the problems raised by the defects in the Articles of Confederation, under which the young nation had been governed—or misgoverned—since the Revolution, while at the same time attempting to create a previously unknown model of ideal government.

This combination of modesty and ambition is understandable if it be borne in mind that, in the eyes of the makers of the Constitution, the main task was as much to create a political system in accord with the eternal nature of man as to reform the confederation. Their "public philosophy" was rooted in a concept of man and his relations with other men which, explicitly or implicitly, always accompanied their thoughts and work. This concept of the nature of man has so thoroughly prevailed, has so intimately shaped the American character and determined the workings of American institutions, and has become so much a part of the American fabric that it is virtually invisible to American eyes. It is, therefore, seldom discussed.

THE shaping of the Constitution started from this question: how does one achieve a "more perfect union" with men who are essentially imperfectible? Man is dominated by his passions, and his passions are dangerously contagious. Society, on the other hand, must be governed by reason. This contradiction between passion and reason is, in effect, the heart of the matter. How is it to be solved? Can man be changed? Should violence be used to oppose his natural human violence, by imposing restraints that domesticate man without necessarily changing his nature? Shall man be changed by curing him of his passions, if need be against his will (the system preferred by rigorous moralists) or by liberating him of obstacles to the legitimate satisfaction of such passions (the procedure favored by utopian socialists)? Or should he, on the contrary, be subordinated to a will that transcends him because it pursues ends unrelated to his own personal happiness yet enables him to achieve happiness through sublimation of his desires (all theories of "the State")?

The key trait of American Constitutional thought is its refusal to accept any one of the imaginable solutions to what is an essentially insoluble problem. It leaves all the questions open: it does not state that there is any pre-established harmony between man and society or between the states and the federal Union, any more than there is a possibility of attaining universal brotherhood. In the view of the Founding Fathers one should not expect more wisdom from a democratic majority than from an opposing minority. Man is by his own nature divided by conflicting passions, just as society, by its nature, is divided into classes and factions of all kinds. For a sovereign authority to attempt to resolve the differences among these divergent groups would be to go against the nature of things and to introduce despotism. Union and concord among men or among the states should not be achieved by imposing consent on them but by establishing a system in which no one possesses any overwhelming degree of power.

If one were required to condense into a single statement the basic concept of freedom incorporated in the Constitution one would say that the guiding idea of the Founding Fathers was to combat evil with evil. They believed that division was a natural fact of life, as evidenced by man's struggle to control his passions. It was also a political fact of life, as evidenced by the strifes and rivalries that had beset the country while it was still a confederation. Moreover, division was inherently an aggressive factor, for they believed that each part of a divided group constantly strives to become the dominant part. This disruptive force was to be counteracted by dispersing the power centers and rendering it impossible for them to combine into a single force. One of the themes most frequently encountered in the Federalist papers is the expression of aversion for what is considered an ideal in many other political systems: the mobilization of wills, followed by a decision reached after mature deliberation.

THE Founders believed in deliberation but not necessarily in the innate wisdom of deliberating bodies. They were inclined to see in every concentration a collusion and in every collusion the seeds of collision. For what really unifies, in their view, is not reason but dedication to a cause, whether individual or collective, whether private or state. Hence their extreme concern to avert pressure by a homogeneous and resolute bloc.

The Constitution, for instance, makes it possible for a citizen to be tried under either federal or state law for the same crime. Thus state and federal authorities can wrangle, as they often do, over their jurisdictions. The whole idea was to atomize, to prevent the coming together of forces, not to promote

IN CONVENTION ASSEMBLED, the Founding Fathers of the American nation meet in Philadelphia in 1787 to frame the U.S. Constitution. After months of deliberation they referred it to the states for ratification; it was adopted on June 21, 1788.

unity. Other artifices were devised to avert "communication and concert [resulting] from the form of government itself." For the Government's task is not to guide the "concert" but much rather to stifle it so that justice may reign—a passive justice whose role was not to reform or improve social conditions but to preserve order and to avoid the supreme injustice: the "enforced equality" often imposed by revolutionary movements. The arsenal of federal enforcement was therefore reduced to a minimum. In fact, the arsenal remained in limbo for a long time, and even after the United States had won two world wars it still had not devised the means for imposing order in a small Southern town except by deploying its war machine.

Yet the spirit of the Constitution is anything but coldly sectional, as is often maintained. Its spirit inclines more toward diffusion than toward strict separatism. The celebrated "separation of powers" is nowhere formulated in absolute terms, nor is its principle an American invention. A great part of the literature bearing on the exalted trinity of executive, legislative and judicial powers rests on pure fiction. In the United States, as elsewhere, the three powers are not "separated" but simply distinguished, with huge overlapping zones.

For example, the Federal Communications Commission and the Federal Trade Commission, both ostensible arms of the executive and both established by the legislature, themselves establish rules (i.e., legislate), see to it that the rules are carried out (i.e., execute), and hold hearings and assign punishments if they are not (i.e., judge). There are other areas of overlapping as well. The concept of autonomous "branches" of government was totally alien to the framers of the Constitution, as were the practices that subsequently became established. The authors of the Constitution sought to neutralize the consolidation of passions, the conspiracy of the mob, as we have noted. They were just as suspicious of the exercise of isolated authority, whether by individuals or administrations. By dispersing and intermixing different powers they hoped to neutralize the danger of individual power and thus to suppress the effect of passions—even at the risk of creating a degree of confusion.

CERTAIN authors actually consider the degree of inconsistency in the functioning of institutions and in the relations among them as a specific virtue of the system. Denis Brogan sees in its relative lack of cohesion a permanent incitement to national unity. American democracy is not a machine that operates on its own. The main function of the Presidency, in fact, is to keep the machine moving, to stimulate Congress, the states, the municipalities and the body politic as a whole to make their own contributions. In contrast to so many other public philosophies, neither clarity nor efficiency is among the values most prized by the American political tradition. It is too suspicious of the intentions and drives that lie behind clarity and efficiency.

Two incidental remarks come to mind. The first is that the complexity and flexibility that the American system manifests behind its solemn façade are not considered drawbacks by Americans. Tocqueville discerned decades ago that Americans feel at ease in its labyrinth, where so many foreign observers get lost. It may even be possible that the archaic contours of the system have enhanced its popularity. For a nation dedicated to adventure and the opening of new lands, these nooks and crannies create a feeling of relaxation and reassurance. The antique is always partly inscrutable, and this is not the least of its attractions. The second observation to be made is that the Constitution was not given once and for all, although it was accepted once and for all; it had to be "reconstituted" every time a difficulty arose. More than once its chief interpreter, the Supreme Court, has dramatically reversed itself, as in 1954 when it overturned the famous "separate but equal" dictum

pronounced in 1896 against early attempts at racial integration. But what lends fascination to the Court's rulings is less its reversals and decisions than its constant despair of reaching "judicially discoverable and manageable standards" valid once and for all—hence its continuous reconsiderations and reappraisals; hence the mounting flow not only of split decisions but of concurring and dissenting opinions, as if each justice's mind were a court in itself.

An abundance of examples of these fluctuations can be found in different fields of litigation, from the recently expanded meaning of the Constitution's "commerce clause" to the shifting doctrines of the justices concerning adoptive citizenship and expatriation, not to speak of even more crucial questions like the scope of the 14th Amendment.

The feeling of basic helplessness in the face of the duty assigned to, or assumed by, the Supreme Court constitutes the rock on which the deep sense of individual responsibility of each justice rests—the stress being on "individual." It was never better expressed than in this statement by Justice Robert H. Jackson in 1948: "It is idle to pretend that this task is one for which we can find in the Constitution one word to help us as judges to decide. . . . Nor can we find guidance in any other legal source. It is a matter on which we can find no law but our own prepossessions." It is evident that the Court is coming to regard itself as a group dedicated, to quote Philip B. Kurland, one of its most learned critics, to the proposition that "if what is unconstitutional is undesirable, then it must be equally true that what is undesirable is unconstitutional." The Court seems increasingly less interested in the guardianship of Constitutional continuity—which would imply a great deal more care and concern for precedents than reflected in Justice Jackson's statement.

A STUDY of the United States' contribution to the political arsenal of our times would show that of the two most original creations it has bequeathed to posterity, one—the Supreme Court—is endowed with an extremely imprecise status, the other—patronage—is without official status at all. Both tend to remove drama from the public scene. This is not to say that the Supreme Court has avoided discussing the most passion-filled issues nor that it has itself been free from prejudice. It has not thrown an impartial and superior light on the debates of the American community, but by taking upon itself the resolution of the passions of its times and turning the debate over them into sophisticated quibbling, it has softened their impact.

While it is not possible to support the argument that the United States has "government by judges," it nevertheless is a fact that American society proportionally includes four times as many lawyers as Great Britain, the country that gave it its original structure. This is because law in the United States is not a uniform rule, but consists of different kinds of law, sometimes competing in irreconcilable fashion.

We thus get the reign of procedure more than the reign of law, and the proliferation of laws and rights leads to the particularization of power, most apparent in the localization of popular representation in the House of Representatives.

THE advantage of this fragmentation of power has been proved by history. The dispersion does not result, as might be concluded from the ideal image of American democracy, in greater security for the individual (judges are not infallible or even incorruptible, and no more curious exception to the "separation of powers" is to be found than the custom of electing rather than appointing judges), although America did manage to avoid those extreme forms of collective oppression to which Europe succumbed. The advantage is of a narrower and more pedestrian nature. Thanks to the number of holes in the social and judicial fabric, it is possible for new claims to obtain recognition. The deliberate imperfections of the system have permitted the imperfect but successful integration of 43 million immigrants, not through the granting of special rights but through what might be designated as a chance of recognition, a chance of advancement. The way patronage enabled the underprivileged to seize, exploit and finally broaden this chance is remarkable.

Thus at the two ends of the American social and institutional ladder, devices have been developed in harmony with the fundamental scheme reflected in the Constitution: at the top is the Supreme Court, which developed in the sense that it determined its own role, breaking free from the tyranny of the evasive clauses that defined its powers; at the bottom is patronage, which was dispensed through political bosses and which absorbed the demands and the possible unrest of waves of newcomers. Both the Court

and patronage tended toward the same goal: to divert the passions, or ambitions, accumulating in the marketplace, the Court acting as a lightning rod, patronage as an irrigation plan, dispersing what potentially could turn into a storm center.

Since the Americans seem enchanted with their institutions, even if they criticize the way they work, and since the institutions, as already noted, are in harmony with the demands of a national growth that undoubtedly would have cracked other political organizations more rigid or more trustful of the nature of man, the question may be asked: how is it that in recent years conferences, seminars and political science studies have been urging a reform—or, at least, pressing for a scrutiny in depth of the American system—and that both newspapers and magazines freely indict the practices and attitudes that the system encourages in Congress and in state assemblies? Has the Constitution run its course and will it be necessary, in the face of incurable excesses, to "rethink" its main features?

THERE are obvious reasons for raising the question, but the answers to the question are not simple. American political organization has indeed been a great experiment, an endeavor to preserve a political system from the demands of politics and from the need for direction. Briefly put, it has been an attempt to dispense with the state, or at least with the apparatus of it, to place people above organization, so as to ensure the coexistence of the members of the society without subjecting them to a superior authority. In this respect, American political history coincides with the evolution of the Presidency. At the beginning the Presidency was conceived of as an institution both exalted and marginal. The President was the Commander in Chief, but he had almost nobody under his orders. What more than anything else changed the center of gravity of the American system —precisely by providing a center of gravity—was the expansion of the central administration under the New Deal. The central administration is still very much fragmented into agencies, but it is becoming increasingly involved in the various sectors of the economic and social life of the nation. Elevated by events to the rank of a great power and then driven by its sheer weight to the position of a superpower, the United States gradually endowed itself with the instruments of intervention, applied both abroad and in the country itself, thus filling the no man's land of the "implicit" attributes of federal power.

The federal Government has not "usurped" anything; it has filled a vacuum. In fact, it may be said that the extension of federal jurisdiction in the course of the past 30 years has provoked only one major conflict: that between the Supreme Court and Franklin D. Roosevelt, which resolved itself.

LISTENING to the partisans of state rights, one might think that the United States, reduced to servitude by federal tutorship, is groaning over its sad fate or desperately resisting Washington's "takeover." But every American citizen can see for himself that this is not so. Every state governor is fired with the ambition to succeed in his administration and will take help where help is available, even from federal funds. Some will do so timidly; others will clamor for more. It is only normal that conflicts should sometimes arise between state and federal authorities. All told, these frictions are negligible, and when they sometimes reach the courts they are seldom of such a dramatic nature (except in the matter of civil rights) as to interest public opinion. Is this the victory of pragmatism over Constitutional talmudism? Yes, to a large extent it is. The same practical and humanitarian needs that unavoidably promote federal responsibility first make themselves felt at the state level. Development of cooperation at the national level is merely a matter of common sense.

The same process by which the federal executive for generations confined itself to purely external affairs (defense, customs, diplomacy) or administrative affairs (national lands, post offices) also took place in the states. Whether "sovereign" or not, the states seldom set up homogeneous and tightly hierarchic governments. They, too, functioned on the basis of a system of dispersed power, and it was through the openings created by this dispersal that the influence of federal power penetrated. It did not have to subjugate or displace any established power; it merely supplemented what was missing. It can be said, therefore, that the American federation does not represent a federal system in the strict sense of the word: the counterpart to the national Government is not necessarily the particular state. The country is not organized that way. When the federal Government takes action it does not necessarily work in concert with an individual state government, as would be the case

in other federal systems. It works just as frequently with municipalities, counties and, increasingly, the great cities, where an ever-larger proportion of the American population is to be found.

It is revealing of this evolution that the U.S. in 1965 established a Cabinet-level Department of Housing and Urban Development and not a Department of Interstate Relations like that of the Federal Republic of Germany, where each state maintains an "embassy" to deal with the central authorities. In American cities—and not only in state capitals—federal buildings are proliferating. Furthermore, it is the populations of the states and not the states themselves that senators now represent in Congress.

The terms in office of senators and the prestige of their offices exceed those of state governors. But in serving their respective states, the senators act exactly as the federal Government acts in its dealings with the states; they seldom go through the "official channels" of the state executive. They have their own channels, their own following, their own means of action. And above all, they are responsible only to the voter, and not to their respective state governments. The decline in the power of the states is in part attributable to the fact that in them the fundamental scheme of the original federal Constitution, with its tendency to favor the dispersal of power and to discourage rational organization, has survived intact. The states in general have failed to amend their own constitutions, leaving themselves in the voluntarily disorganized pattern of the 19th Century.

ONE can dilute power, but one cannot dissolve human masses once they have settled and multiplied in a place. And the same holes in the sociopolitical structure that in the past allowed political machines and patronage to work positively are today not large enough to enable vast sections of the population to move upward. These are the subcitizens rooted in destitution, too apathetic or estranged from the society to build anything but an accumulation of wild resentments. Fortunately, that group's potential for violence has never been triggered on a large scale, partly because of the restrictions inherent in the fundamental pattern of the American system. That potential nevertheless remains a danger. Deprivation of rights and dignity does not always disturb the surface. But as was shown by the incredibly widespread and lively response that the reapportionment decision of 1962 met from the lower courts and from suit-filing citizens eager to catch up at once with decades of malapportionment, still waters should not be trusted for too long.

This reversal of the original intent of the Constitution's authors may be observed in other and more important fields. The role of the President has become dominant. Press and television every day focus attention on his acts and gestures. The White House now sends to Congress completely drafted legislative proposals each time a matter of national interest is involved, and the "legislators" can only obstruct them or amend them. For its part, the Supreme Court more and more abstains from passing judgment on the constitutionality of laws and concentrates on problems relating to the protection of individual freedoms. Congress reacts to its loss of initiative and to the obscurity that surrounds its proceedings with a show of greater "vigilance" over the various sectors of the Administration, almost without ever participating in the elaboration of their policies. The very concepts of executive and legislative branches, not to mention more general notions such as checks and balances, have lost some of their precision. As far as it is still possible, the problem is only to "check" the White House.

IT is obvious that American institutions and the forces they are supposed to control have for some time been entering a new phase, which for lack of a better term might be called extraconstitutional. Unheard-of interpretations of the Constitution are being explored. Yet no absolutely conclusive lessons have been drawn. On the contrary, questions about what should be reshaped or corrected are on the increase. As underlined in a recent study of this question, there is "the difficulty of assessing the likely outcomes of a given proposal for change. It is this uncertainty that intervenes between the perception of problems and agreement on solutions, even when there is no disagreement on goals." To all appearances, the present climate is conducive neither to an overhaul on the scale of the great Legislative Reorganization Act of 1946 nor to reform through Constitutional amendment. What should be aimed at? A state of "no disagreement on goals" has yet to be reached. Diagnosis of the ailment varies with the patient's health. What looked incurable under President John F. Kennedy briefly receded under President Lyndon B. Johnson. A new series of studies will be necessary to determine the nature of the supposed illness plaguing the illustrious patient: the American system.

But there is at least one good reason for not expecting important changes in the style of political life or in the functioning of the nation's institutions. This reason holds good despite the adjustments that might follow the likely emergence of the federal civil service as another force on the scene. The rise of the federal bureaucracy will in itself greatly modify the U.S. political landscape, even if nothing official will be done to recognize or sanction the existence of this new giant. On the contrary, one can assume that the feeling that there will be changes in this direction will dampen for the moment any eagerness for alteration in the over-all system. After all, American politicians are more at home with the spirit of wheeling and dealing than with that of dynamic discipline.

THEY find stimulation in the apparent disorder of the American political landscape, in its intersecting lines and in its overlapping perspectives. Where foreign politicians would first think, "Let us smooth, let us harmonize all this," the U.S. politician will tell himself, "I'll take care of it"—especially if he is sitting in the White House. And it will be a point of honor for him to prove that he is as good at moving around an obstacle as at overcoming it.

Often a simple idea suffices to counteract a habit. Is it not the practice for the President, just as for a prime minister in a purely parliamentary regime, to intervene in person in Congress? If he deems it useful, he will invite a large number of congressmen to the drawing rooms of the White House and there explain his policies to them. The congressmen will go as to a reception, not as to a working session; but they will bring to the reception the same serious spirit, though not the same attitude of mind, that they bring to Congressional debates.

This improvising empiricism has spared the American democracy the disasters suffered by other democracies. It has become a part of American life, shaping generation after generation. Other generations will follow which, imbued with this legacy, will in turn aspire to clarifying and modernizing the American political system by effecting rational regroupings. For, by a providential grace, the Founding Fathers never dispensed the people from bringing to life creative sons and grandsons.

TAKING ACTION, a church-led civil rights group marches on the Washington State Capitol in Olympia. The marchers were demonstrating in favor of a bill that would outlaw discrimination in housing.

DISCUSSING STRATEGY at the Washington State House of Representatives, a lobbyist *(facing the house chamber)* confers with three men whom he has lined up to testify on the advisability of a tax bill.

Opinions are polled in a Democratic caucus room during a session led by House Speaker Robert Schaefer (background, with hand raised).

Vigorous Democracy Working at the Local Level

Few areas of American life are unaffected by the presence of the federal Government. Yet, because of the immense size of the system, national leaders are often remote from the day-to-day lives of their constituents. But on the local levels, where many of the same forces that animate the federal Government are at work, the immediacy of issues and the accessibility of politicians generate participation by the people. The Puget Sound city of Olympia, Washington, shown here and on the following pages as it was in the mid-1960s, is a model of meshing systems of government. As state capital, county seat and self-governing city, Olympia reflects a democratic tradition: citizens making and enforcing their own laws.

CLOSE TO HOME, city and county officials in Olympia remain accessible to the people whom they serve

THE CITY FATHERS gather at the 10-acre site *(right)* of Olympia's new city hall to inspect plans for a modern building to replace the city's old municipal offices.

A LESSON IN DEMOCRACY is given to 4-H Club members by Commissioner George F. Yantis Jr. *(foreground)* as he helps them "run" the county for a day.

MUNICIPAL AFFAIRS, open to public scrutiny, are conducted in the city's police courtroom at meetings presided over by Mayor Neil R. McKay *(above, far left).*

A TRAFFIC VIOLATOR, standing before Judge Doane Brodie, is tried in the same courtroom. The court holds evening sessions to accommodate working defendants.

LEGISLATIVE PROCESSES involve debate and compromise, and pressure by lobbyists

CIVIL RIGHTS ADVOCATES, led by Rev. Paul Beeman, a registered lobbyist *(above, left)*, sing "We Shall Overcome" as they enter the Capitol rotunda to push a fair-housing bill.

INTERESTED CITIZEN, cattleman Henry J. Schnebly *(above, left)* discusses a property tax bill with a lobbyist in "Ulcer Gulch," a balcony area between the two legislative chambers.

POWERFUL GROUP, the state senate rules committee *(r.* meets to consider the bill wanted by the civil rights march The committee decided to keep the bill from the senate fl

FLOOR CONFERENCE brings state Representative Eric Braun, a Democrat *(below, standing),* across the aisle to talk over a proposed bill with two Republican members of the house.

A YOUNG GOVERNOR, Dan Evans is a Republican with enough political appeal to have won in a Democratic year

POSING FOR PICTURES after signing a bill, Governor Evans surrounds himself with members of the state legislature who were instrumental in getting the bill through the house and senate.

MEETING THE PRESS, articulate Governor Evans replies to reporters' questions in his portrait-hung office *(right)*. The Governor likes to talk of national and foreign affairs as well as state matters.

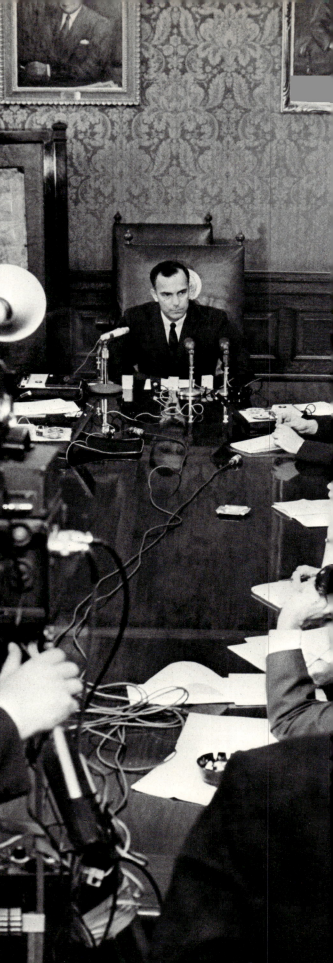

ENTERTAINING AT HOME, Governor Evans, his wife Nancy and her brother, Bill Bell, an official concerned with Washington's trade, discuss a projected trip to Japan to visit a trade fair. Even at home the Evanses seldom escape state business.

HOLDING A DINNER just before leaving on a skiing vacation, the Evanses *(at head and foot of table)* laugh with a group of close friends. The Governor is an avid and expert skier and sailor and has climbed most of Washington's highest mountains.

MAJESTIC AIR of the Washington state buildings echoes that of Washington, D.C.

STATE LIBRARY looks out on Washington's handsome Capitol *(left)*. The library serves the same purpose as the federal Government's Library of Congress, performing reference services for the legislators and housing the state's official files.

STATELY ROTUNDA of the Washington Capitol is visited by tourists, who inspect the rope-encircled state seal *(left)*. Because of the remarkable acoustic properties of the rotunda, organ concerts often are held for the enjoyment of visitors.

HOUSE GALLERY is packed with citizens *(below)* who have come to watch hearings on a tax bill. School children often attend hearings. When a group arrives, their local legislator frequently introduces them and the other lawmakers applaud.

An Economy Born of Democracy

by MASSIMO SALVADORI

AMERICAN economic achievement is one of the impressive realities of the modern world. Communities that had started from nothing and that for a long time were truly underdeveloped were by the middle of the 18th Century causing foreign observers to marvel at the progress that had been made in America through ingenuity and energy. Since Independence the United States has been a world leader in per capita production of goods and services and in standards of living, as well as in economic inventiveness and experimentation. Since World War I the American nation has led, too, in what matters most to humanity: the ability to help others generously and the willingness to do so.

On the North Atlantic seaboard the early settlers found neither lush terrain such as that of the West Indies nor economically developed areas such as there were in the viceroyalties of New Spain and Peru. Many generations went by before the fertile plains of the Midwest were reached, and more still before any appreciable mineral wealth was discovered. In much of the West the settlers found greater obstacles of all kinds than were met by colonists elsewhere in the Western Hemisphere. Thus neither empty spaces nor natural resources explain why tens of millions of immigrants came to the United States instead of going to other parts of the world just as empty and with as many resources.

This colossal migration, the largest and most beneficial in history, happened because of the American economic system. Some immigrants were looking for liberty, but most were simply looking for a livelihood, and with a few exceptions they came without capital and with little technical skill. Now their descendants are living an infinitely better life than their cousins do in the old countries. Settlement, expansion, vast immigration, the rise from nothing to the world's most prosperous nation—all this can be summed up in one word: progress. It has not been steady. There have been ups and downs. Prophets of doom have often announced with relish the end of the American free enterprise system. Instead, after each reverse there has been a resurgence and a leap forward.

The United States occupies about one fifteenth of the world's land area. Its citizens account for not quite one fifteenth of all mankind. But the American economy produces about one third of all the goods produced in the world and a still higher percentage of services. The United States uses more than one third of all the energy consumed in the world. American manufacturing leads that of all other nations, as it has since it overtook British industrial production in the 19th Century. Living standards are related chiefly to the supply of utilities and services; on both counts the United States exceeds every other nation. Agriculture is a small sector of the American economy, but it looms large in relation to the rest of the world, contributing, for instance, about one fifth of the world's output of the six main grains and of meats. Labor productivity is high and capital is efficiently managed, as proved by the ratio between production on one hand and labor and capital on the other.

The large output of goods and services is related to the ability to expand—the dynamic drive characteristic of the American economy. In both absolute and relative terms the expansion since Independence has been greater than in any other country. Only for short periods have other national economies done as well, and seldom better. In the first 100 years after Independence the developed wealth of the United States—the collective riches of the nation—increased 37-fold. During the last 100 years family incomes, in terms of goods and services used, have increased sevenfold, while the population has expanded about 600 per cent: this makes a 42-fold increase in total personal incomes. The expansion continues. Between 1965 and 1967 both gross national product and total personal incomes increased about 15 per cent. From 1961 to the end of 1967, 12 million additional jobs in industry were created. Over this same period eight million families achieved yearly incomes above $10,000.

EXPANSION has been accomplished by change in the products as well as in the processes of production and distribution. Economic change in the United States has always been rapid and often radical. In its wake have been the ruins of obsolete activities and the insecurity of many who could not adapt themselves, but the over-all picture is one of astounding forward movement. Examples of recent change go all the way from the replacement of natural raw materials with synthetic ones to the substitution of automated machines for human labor and man-operated machines. Change has been the result of the drive for profits, efficiency and reduced costs. It was made possible by inventions, which have been abundant because man's creativity has been stimulated by a favorable social environment. Vast financial resources have helped to produce inventions: $60 billion was spent on scientific research and development in the 1950s; more than twice that much will probably have been spent in the 1960s.

The high level of production, the continued expansion and the constant change have for a long time been features of the American economy. As a result the entire economic system has undergone deep transformations. The present variety of American free enterprise differs from previous ones and from those existing in other countries. It is sometimes called neocapitalism, social capitalism or people's capitalism, but names matter little: what count

MASSIMO SALVADORI, who was born in London in 1908 of Anglo-Italian parents and brought up in Florence, graduated from the University of Geneva in 1929 and received a doctorate in political science from the University of Rome in 1930. Since coming to the U.S. in 1938, he has taught at St. Lawrence University, Bennington College and Smith College, where he is now Professor of History. His lifelong interest in the U.S., its government and its economy is reflected in his book *The Economics of Freedom*.

are the system's distinctive elements. Considering the number of people having a voice in the economic process through their ability to decide such things as what to produce, what to consume or how much to work, the American economic system is the most democratic of any in a major country. Authoritarian tendencies are inherent in all economies in which public or private capital plays a dominant role. But in the American free enterprise economy these tendencies have been curbed by forces operating within the system and working toward improving it. The improvement has been effected through diffusion of ownership of the means of production and exchange, by wide participation in what economists call the policy-making process (the sum of decisions affecting the economy), by emphasis on consumer spending and by a gradual reduction in the range of average incomes of the various sectors of the population.

Even in its restricted meaning of developed productive capital—i.e., what is used to produce goods and services—property is remarkably widely diffused in the United States. In 1965 about 10 million Americans owned unincorporated enterprises and more than 20 million shared in the ownership of corporate securities. The two figures overlap somewhat, but one may fairly say that an exceptionally large percentage of American families shares directly or indirectly in the ownership of the means of production and exchange. Again in 1965, millions of other Americans owned property in the form of savings accounts, insurance policies, homes and valuable durable goods. For hundreds of thousands of independent professional and semiprofessional people, property consisted not only of equipment but also of skills acquired through expensive training.

WHERE the policy-making process is concerned there is no small group in the United States today with the power to make arbitrary economic decisions. Even in the case of large corporations, with billions in assets, controlling a large share of a given market, managers and directors must take into account stockholders, employees who may strike and consumers who may decide to buy someone else's product. The freedom of individual entrepreneur or manager is effectively limited by the choices Americans have as producers, as consumers and as citizens. The possibility of making a choice is constantly present, even if many people do not take advantage of it—if they are satisfied with what they have or at least unwilling to make an effort to change. Choice is possible not only because the economy is vast and highly differentiated, but also because capital and labor at all levels are fluid and enjoy great mobility.

CONSUMPTION by the people, not by the state or by parasitic privileged classes, is of course the proper goal of economic activities in any democratic society. In the United States the priority of the people as consumers is not a matter of debate; it is taken for granted, even if the troubled international situation has compelled Americans since 1948 to devote a large part of their productive activity to military preparedness. Increasing production of goods and services and new products has led to changes in family budgets. Recent changes, particularly, are indicative of steadily rising standards of living. Spending for food is down to about one fifth of the average family budget, from about two fifths in 1948. Expenses for education, for participation in civic and religious affairs, and for leisure now account for more than one tenth of the average family budget; housing (purchase or rent, maintenance, furnishings, utilities) has gone up from a little over one fourth of the family budget in 1948 to nearly one third. The average American home is more spacious than those of all but two or three other countries; utilities and laborsaving household devices are more abundant; and the ratio of occupants to the number of rooms available is among the lowest.

Of great importance for the democratization of the American economy is the trend toward a narrower range of incomes. There still is considerable poverty at the bottom of American society, and there are huge fortunes at the top. Poverty is a problem—even if Franklin D. Roosevelt's famous "one third of a nation ill-housed, ill-clad and ill-nourished" of 1937 had been reduced to less than one fifth by 1965, and even if among the poor are included many who elsewhere would be considered well-to-do. For several decades the range of incomes has been narrowing, while at the same time there has been a rapid general upward movement. Between 1941 and 1963 the increase of average incomes, measured in terms of goods and services purchased, was 79 per cent for the lowest fifth of the population and only 30 per cent for the top 5 per cent of the population. The number of families in the middle-income groups has increased steadily: in 1947 families with incomes in the $5,000-$10,000 range (in dollars of equivalent purchasing power) made up 29 per cent of the total, while in 1962 they made up 43 per cent. Fiscal measures that deprive the well-to-do of part of their income and social services and benefits that help the less well-to-do both contribute to the leveling off of incomes. Instead of the traditional pyramidal society, with a small number of wealthy persons at the top and a mass of poor at the bottom, a diamond-shaped society is evolving in the United States. Both the top and the bottom have shrunk; most of the people are in the middle.

One more feature of America's variety of the free enterprise system is worth mentioning. Lincoln once observed that among Americans "a considerable number of persons mingle their own labor with capital." He was referring of course to the fact that a large percentage of the nation was then composed of independent farmers and small businessmen who applied their labor to the capital they owned. The mingling is still there, although of a different nature. More and more people are employees, while at the same time more and more own property from which they receive an income that is added to the income received in the form of salaries, wages and bonuses. This mingling blurs the traditional distinction between those who derive their income from capital and those who derive it from labor. The American nation, with its tens of millions of people who work and own property, is the antithesis both of the traditional societies divided into those who own and those who work and of the collectivist societies in which all citizens are employees and lack the independence given by property.

FROM the gigantic output of goods and services to the remarkable degree of economic democracy, the American economic system has distinctive features. Why the distinctiveness? It does not derive from the essential elements of the American economic mechanism—the search for high remuneration of capital and labor in a system of competitive markets and prices modified by Government action —because these elements also exist in other and different free enterprise systems abroad. The distinctiveness is not in the physical environment, which is no better or worse than in areas of comparable size in other parts of the world. Nor is it to be found in basic wants and drives, which are more or less the same for all human beings.

The distinctiveness of the American economy is related first of all to the American Way of Life. It derives from values and ideas that are prevalent in the American culture today—and were prevalent for a long time during the formative period of the nation. The economic tone was set by a body of citizens —not necessarily ever a majority—whose values and ideas led them to create the institutions characteristic of the American economy. The institutions in turn molded the rest of the nation.

WHAT the American economic institutions are is well known—from the stock market and the labor unions to the federal regulatory agencies and business organizations. There is less awareness of the values and ideas that made for these—the key elements in the ethical and conceptual framework prevalent among influential sections of the American nation. Rugged individualism is part of the American myth, although actually there has been less of it than many think: beginning with New England Puritans and Virginia planters and coming all the way down to 20th Century corporation managers and economic committees at all levels, teamwork and collaboration have been important features of American economic life. Even so, individualism has played a stimulating role in the American economy. American culture has made the individual responsible for his actions and thus has promoted his independence and his initiative.

No less important has been the role of the basic ideas and the method of thinking that have been prevalent for a long time in the American nation. The conceptual framework that set the tone for the nation was a type of undogmatic rationalism: as such it has been forward-looking, exploratory, experimental and pragmatic. It has made the fullest use of the scientific method, the method that best helps man to achieve control over nature.

Next in importance to individualism and undogmatic rationalism has been a belief in the dignity of work, a value despised or ignored by the majority of human beings. Work, however humble, was held in high esteem among early American settlers. For many generations this produced a widespread compulsion to be active, to have a career—even when this was not strictly necessary. Gentlemen of leisure, parasites and idlers there have always been, but they have remained fringe elements, extraneous to the mainstream of American life. The stress on work was linked to materialism, a term, for most, with unpleasant connotations. But materialism, the search for a more comfortable life on the part of millions, has been a major element in inducing those millions to make the extra effort needed for passing from a stagnant and therefore restricted economy to a dynamic and affluent one. A strong belief in success as something worth aiming at also pushed people to work hard.

The sense of individual autonomy and responsibility fostered an attachment to liberty, stimulating millions of Americans in all generations to lead independent lives, to start independent careers, and to rely primarily on themselves rather than on their family, their friends, the community or the state. It also stimulated Americans to agitate for their individual rights, which they understood to include the right to get the maximum return for their labor, their skills or their capital.

FINALLY, with the exception of the psychological and institutional barriers against the colored minority, in most of America there was enough sense of equality to eliminate the obstacle to improvement represented by the privileges of the upper classes and the docility of lower ones.

None of the above-mentioned values and ideas has ever held total sway in the American nation. These qualities have, however, been sufficiently widespread to provide the foundation of what has long been called the American system of guided private enterprise. Small business has at various times curbed the power of big business, indebted entrepreneurs have curbed banking corporations, farmers have curbed railroad corporations, organized employees have curbed management and consumers have curbed producers. Government—i.e., the citizens acting through their elected representatives—has intervened to correct the imbalance brought by the pressure of one or another economic force, by technological changes or simply by modifications in the economic process. Jacksonianism checked the power of early financiers, and Populism and Progressivism led the agitation for reforms that limited monopolies and ended the short-lived era of the Robber Barons.

In the 20th Century the Square Deal and the New Freedom, through the New and Fair Deals, led to the New Frontier and the Great Society.

These changes have meant that instead of liberty as anarchy there has been liberty under law. The number of new business enterprises every year, the disappearance of others, mergers and liquidations, mobility of capital and labor, price fluctuations—all these indicate that economic liberty is a reality in the United States. The ambitious, energetic individual who prefers independent economic activity to private or public employment can set up his own enterprise. He will find obstacles, but wherever he starts, at the bottom of the economic ladder or farther up, the difficulties are probably no greater than they were 100 years ago.

AT the same time there are now well-defined limits to economic liberty. Ever since the Union was formed, and a single economic market thereby created, the overwhelming majority of civically minded Americans has agreed that a self-regulating market economy gives far better results and is fairer to everyone, or anyhow to most, than authoritarian command economies. Within that majority many have wanted the absolute freedom that politically means anarchy and leads to despotism and economically means excessive instability and, through crises and depressions, leads to a system of monopolies.

Others—sometimes a majority, the rest of the time a large, articulate minority—have agreed instead that government should correct the defects of the economic system, should provide stimuli to achieve greater business activity and greater purchasing power, and—more recently—should help those who are left behind in the economic race. From Hamilton's advocacy of protectionism to President Johnson's Great Society, supporters of government action have opposed supporters of integral laissez faire. The former have been successful to the extent that American economic freedom is now the outcome of laws aimed at maintaining and expanding the field of economic activities within which the citizens can give rein to their capacity for independent action.

Liberty under law has given American corporations their distinctive characteristics. The attention of the public, of public-opinion molders, of politicians and of economists is usually focused on big business, on the relatively small number of gigantic enterprises; however, from the point of view of the economic system and its contribution to progress through inventiveness, innovation, experimentation, and technological and managerial efficiency, the whole range of enterprises, from minuscule to giant, plays a role. In 1967 there were more than 1.4 million active incorporated businesses in the United States, nearly one tenth of all enterprises. From these came more than three fifths of the total output of goods and services. They were the chief source of capital formation, carried the main responsibility for the expansion of the economy and contributed about one fourth of all federal receipts in 1967.

Today's corporations are a new breed. Diffusion of ownership is a fast-growing phenomenon, largely owing to a conscious policy of corporation managers, who realize that the wider the ownership the greater is the public's stake in maintaining a system in which corporations flourish. The diffusion of ownership of corporations contributes in a free enterprise industrial society to the social stability that in agrarian societies is achieved through the diffusion of land ownership. Management is more and more divorced from ownership. The managerial class is large and attracts many of the more dynamic and better-educated people in the nation. The new salaried managerial class has, on the whole, a more comprehensive, broader and more long-range view of the economy than the former class of managing owners. Its members find a large turnover with a small margin of profit more advantageous than higher profits on a smaller turnover; they are concerned with price stability and the purchasing power of the public; they are aware of the importance of scientific research and invest large sums in expanding and equipping scientific laboratories; they give capital formation priority over payment of dividends; and they encourage both short- and long-term planning.

WHILE ownership has spread, management nevertheless has become more concentrated. The diffusion of economic power derived from property ownership, a development that is favorable to liberty, is accompanied by the centralization of economic activities necessary to efficiency and favorable to expansion. Except in a few cases concentration has not created monopolistic or even near-monopolistic situations. Corporation managers operate under the control and stimulus of actual or potential

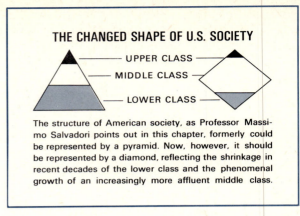

THE CHANGED SHAPE OF U.S. SOCIETY

UPPER CLASS
MIDDLE CLASS
LOWER CLASS

The structure of American society, as Professor Massimo Salvadori points out in this chapter, formerly could be represented by a pyramid. Now, however, it should be represented by a diamond, reflecting the shrinkage in recent decades of the lower class and the phenomenal growth of an increasingly more affluent middle class.

competition. No branch of economic activity in the United States is independent from others: for example, concentration is high in the automobile industry, but this is subject to the pressures exercised by the rapid expansion of air transportation, by choked roads and by the importing of foreign cars. In the American economy as a whole, competition continues to play its role of stimulating improvement and weeding out inefficiency.

On the basis of published reports corporate profits in the United States are impressive and often look astronomical. Actually they are on the whole far from astronomical. During the prosperous early 1960s about three fifths of all corporations showed a profit, while the others took losses. Deducting federal and other taxes (which absorb about half of the gross profits) and reinvestments, profits in the early 1960s amounted to 3 or 4 per cent of all business receipts and contributed only about 4 per cent to personal incomes.

Among the negative elements in today's corporate structure are the excessive bigness of some corporations, the lingering tendency toward monopolistic practices, and bureaucratism. What the best size is for any enterprise cannot be scientifically established, but there is a point beyond which bigness becomes unmanageable and leads to inefficiency. In recent years some large corporations have adopted a policy of decentralization in order to maintain efficiency. As monopoly is the easy way to compensate for inefficiency, monopolistic tendencies are permanently present and the curbing of them is one of the major economic responsibilities of the federal Government. Red tape, waste caused by personal rivalries, the slowing down of those persons—from bench workers to executives—who have achieved tenure and are no longer sufficiently motivated—these are some of the defects of all bureaucratic organizations, private as well as public. The line separating a satisfactory performance from an unsatisfactory one is thin, but the American corporate structure in general has remained on the right side of it.

Labor—not just the wage earners but all whose income derives from their own exertions more than from capital—has contributed not less than corporations to changes in the American economic system. In the early years tariffs were sought more by the section of the labor force composed of self-employed industrial producers, who were then many, than by capitalists, who were few. Federal and state initiative in developing transportation facilities was sought early in the 19th Century by independent producers and by prospective producers who were intent on moving west. Self-employed labor in agriculture and industry was largely responsible for the election in 1828 and 1832 of Andrew Jackson, the spokesman for what some already were calling democratic capitalism. The agitation of industrial employed labor and of agricultural self-employed labor was a major factor in the economic legislation of the 1880s and 1890s. Industrial employed labor was one of the pillars on which the New Deal was built. The successful agitation for higher pay on the part of all sectors of the labor force helped solve the problems of surplus production during periods of prosperity and of unemployment in periods of depression—problems that had baffled economists, the business community and politicians alike.

CONTRARY to what was once the case in the United States and still is in most societies, there is relatively little difference between the earnings of self-employed labor and the earnings of employees. In 1964 the average earnings for nonagricultural self-employed labor was about $6,000, for agricultural self-employed labor about $3,000. For employees, annual remuneration was close to $5,400 in industry and to $2,500 (including housing) in farming. Class tension, the scourge of most nations, has been lessened in the United States by the fact that all self-employed, all salaried personnel and the majority of wage earners consider themselves members of the middle class. The minority of wage earners who still think of themselves as working class shrinks as wages increase, tenure becomes less precarious and

long-term contracts replace short-term ones. Economically and psychologically, America has become overwhelmingly a middle-class society.

Most of the labor force supports the fundamental institutions and principles of the American economic system. This is true not only of the self-employed and higher-paid employees but also of millions of salaried personnel and wage earners organized in labor unions. Shortly after the merger in 1955 of the older American Federation of Labor and the more recent Congress of Industrial Organizations, creating the joint AFL-CIO, an official statement made three points: the interests of labor and management are interdependent; free labor, as much as free capitalistic enterprise, requires a free government; American labor relies on collective bargaining and on strikes, not on extension of Government controls, to achieve its aims of higher living standards and economic security. These points have remained the foundation of the policies of American labor unions, whose influence is considerable in the decisions taken by corporations, in shaping economic and social legislation, and in aiding democratic labor organizations in other countries.

THE total laissez faire advocated by 19th Century classical economists found relatively few partisans in the United States, where the view that the economy functions within a frame of laws had usually prevailed. Concerning the Government's economic role, Americans have tried to stay close to the teachings of the 18th Century British economist Adam Smith, who, sounder than his disciples, wrote in *The Wealth of Nations:* "The sovereign has . . . the duty of protecting, as far as possible, every member of the society from the injustice or oppression of every other member of it . . . and . . . the duty of erecting and maintaining certain public works and certain public institutions, which it can never be for the interest of any individual, or small number of individuals, to erect and maintain."

In the first decades of the Union, public action in the United States was concerned mainly with the distribution of unoccupied land, the creation of a transportation system and the protection of the American market against external economic pressure. Later on, public action began to deal with the curbing of financial monopolies. During the last three generations to the curbing of monopolies was added the curbing of powerful industrial trusts and, more recently, of labor unions bent on gaining a privileged position.

The business cycle, unemployment, productivity and even runaway economic growth—the last being of special concern because it affects not only prosperity but also military strength—have been some of the problems leading to greater Government intervention in the economy. Adam Smith's "public works" would today include the development of nuclear energy, basic scientific research and space exploration. These are three fields in which the American Government has been increasingly active in recent years. As time goes on and the economy expands, the range and scope of "public works" is likely to increase. This does not necessarily mean a reduction in the range and scope of private enterprise: a comparison of the 1960s with the 1920s shows that greater Government action has not caused a shrinking of private activities or made them less profitable. If the pie is bigger, all slices can be larger.

THE federal Government reaches into myriad activities through the Antitrust Division of the Department of Justice, through various divisions of the Department of Labor, the Federal Reserve System, the Social Security Administration, many other federal regulatory agencies (AEC, CAB, FCA and the like), and the armed forces. Early in 1965 the federal Government owned and managed more than 20,000 commercial enterprises. From the Land Act of 1800 to the Employment Act of 1946 and more recent legislation, Congress (along with the Supreme Court and state legislatures) has created the legal frame within which the astounding expansion of the American economy has taken place. In the course of six generations since the Union came into existence, many errors have naturally been made by federal and state authorities, but the outcome shows that right decisions have outweighed wrong ones.

The legislation of the past third of a century has helped to shape the present form of American free enterprise. In the early 1930s the insecurity of tens of millions of Americans deriving from the instability of the economic system was the problem overshadowing all others. The American nation was dangerously close to the point beyond which uncertainty becomes unendurable. Personal insecurity was

at first lessened by various emergency measures until a comprehensive federal social security system was established, augmented by state action and by a large number of efficient plans evolved through private initiative. Federal social security now covers most of the population and accounts for a steadily increasing proportion of personal incomes. In 1966 about $39 billion was paid by the federal Government for old-age and disability pensions, for public assistance and for unemployment compensation.

SINCE the 1930s the instability of the economic system has been greatly reduced through the introduction of a number of so-called stabilizers. During the last quarter of a century there has not been a single major economic or financial crisis in the United States, only a few minor recessions. The evidence shows that Americans are well on the way to controlling the business cycle. Social security is one of the stabilizers. Another is social services, now being greatly expanded. Elementary and secondary public education—largely the responsibility of local and state government—cost in the middle 1960s about $20 billion, representing an average annual expenditure of nearly $500 per pupil. Even before the passing of federal legislation in 1965, public medical care cost close to six billion dollars. A third major stabilizer is farm price supports to aid the troubled farming community. The federal farm subsidy program cost around five billion dollars in 1964.

The economy is kept on an even keel by the varying level of public spending that neutralizes fluctuations in purchasing power; by fiscal policies —such as the 1964 and 1965 tax reductions—that take more and more into account the over-all economic picture and are the result of careful scientific planning; by selective controls that regulate credit; by low-interest federal loans affecting small business and housing construction; by public works, including in recent years the new highway system being built largely with federal funds. Orderly growth benefiting all sectors of the population is the aim of the President's Council of Economic Advisers, the agency responsible for suggesting appropriate economic, financial and fiscal measures.

Economic growth in the U.S. has had a wide-ranging influence both internally and externally. It has made possible the swift expansion of already vast establishments of educational, scientific, religious, recreational and other cultural activities. It has provided the American nation with more professional and semiprofessional people, more writers, artists and scientists than there are, relative to the population, in any other nation. The American economy supports public services that in 1965 cost all together close to $200 billion and employed more than 10 million people. It has enabled the United States Government to donate in two decades more than $100 billion to other countries, while at the same time citizens have privately helped foreign nations to the tune of several billions more. Other national economies have been stimulated by nearly $70 billion invested privately in foreign countries and by about $40 billion worth of foreign trade annually. American industry was a major factor in winning World War I and World War II for the Allies and in holding back the expansionist drives of Stalinist and Maoist Communism. American agriculture has since World War II been a major factor in checking starvation in European, Asian and North African countries ravaged by wars and civil wars or brought to the brink of famine by the population explosion.

IN the American environment the expanding free enterprise economy means greater independence for individuals and groups. Conformity, group pressures, repressive and oppressive mores are part of American life as they are of the life of all nations. But dissenters of all kinds can find more easily than elsewhere the resources that enable them to stand for what they believe to be right. This applies to integrationists struggling for civil rights, to avant-garde writers and artists, to educators experimenting with unconventional educational systems. The resulting independence of individuals and groups is valuable: it also makes, of course, for considerable unrest and tension.

Americans are better fed, clothed and housed than ever before. New generations grow taller. There are increasing opportunities for rest and relaxation. There are more museums, concert halls, libraries, colleges, research institutes and scientific laboratories. More records and books are sold. More people travel. But material abundance also has its debit side. It means, for example, a large and growing market for liquor and for pornographic publications. Asocial and amoral behavior is stimulated because of too much money and too much leisure among many who have little or no sense of responsibility. Since regular work often helps to keep people on an even keel emotionally and mentally, less work contributes to the growing rate of personal instability. The problems created by affluence are many.

Dissatisfaction and tension related to economic problems are sometimes greater in the United States than in countries where change is less rapid, the level of output lower, unevenness of distribution greater, and economic stability and security less. In fairness one should recognize the role of noneconomic factors in this situation. In the United States freedom of expression and of debate and the abundance of communication media increase awareness of problems and heighten tension correspondingly. Poverty, slums, unequal incomes and many other defects may actually amount to less in the United States than in most other countries, but since Americans are more aware of them they complain more loudly. Many of the poor would be considered well-to-do in other countries, but they are more resentful of their poverty than the poor of other nations. Among the American well-to-do, those who do not restrict their wants and desires find it as difficult to live within an income of $20,000 as to live within the limits of a smaller income. Americans are discovering that standards of living are not necessarily related to happiness.

Even discounting the effects of freedom of expression and debate, of negativeness and of emotionalism, the problems facing America's economy are many. Rapid change makes them more acute. Variations in price and wage levels, unemployment due to technological transformation, strikes, speculation, steady depreciation of the currency and many other problems remain manageable only as long as they are kept within relatively narrow bounds. The larger the economy, the greater is the need for a strong institutional structure to keep it stable.

WHATEVER the defects of the American economic system, the evidence indicates that so far it has benefited its own people and millions abroad more than any other economic system has ever done. It is likely to continue to do so for a long time to come, provided there is sound management at both the private and the public level.

A BUSY COMPUTER SALESMAN, Gary Cadwallader *(above, right)*, who covers the Minneapolis-St. Paul area for International Business Machines, explains new I.B.M. equipment in the already computerized offices of a farm equipment firm. Trained in engineering, Cadwallader was given additional instruction by I.B.M. in arcane fields such as systems design.

AN EXPERT TECHNICIAN, Cadwallader sells his computers with the aid of blackboard talks. Salesmen of such complex machines must know how their product can help each customer.

The Changing Pattern of the Nation's Life

The swift growth and the constantly changing pattern of the United States economy are radically altering the lives of millions of Americans. Men earn their livings in ways that would have been inconceivable a few years ago, or use daring new techniques to streamline older operations. The fear that automation would create mass unemployment is being modified by the realization that technological progress often creates new jobs. As menial work is eliminated, new skills come into play, leisure increases, and the economy prospers. The computer has not just helped solve mathematics problems: it is well on the way to altering the whole fabric of American life.

AMPLE LEISURE HOURS afforded by his specialized work allow Cadwallader to take his wife and son for a boat ride (*right*) on a lake that is just behind their modern home.

WOMAN AT WORK, Mrs. Robert L. Lambert,
one of three million women with professional
or technical jobs, doubles as hematologist and housewife

AT THE BLOOD BANK at Temple University Hospital in Philadelphia, Mrs. Lambert, known professionally as Dr. Lyndall Molthan, inspects a pint of blood.

IN THEIR YARD, Mrs. Lambert and her husband, Dr. Robert L. Lambert, a prominent chest specialist and teacher, relax in the sun and read the Sunday newspaper.

IN HER KITCHEN, Mrs. Lambert gives her three daughters ice-cream sticks after lunch. Despite her professional duties, she has time for fun with her children.

ON AN EXCURSION through the Pennsylvania countryside, the Lamberts drive their spruced-up antique car, a classic 1934 Packard complete with rumble seat.

81

Hard working Wesley R. Brush, a market and product planning manager of the Buick Division of General Motors, pores over charts on a Satur

TRAVELING ON BUSINESS, Brush flies from Chicago to Flint with a toy animal for his son. Brush is away from home about five days a month.

TRAINING COURSE for Buick executives is attended by Brush *(right, at end of table)*. Most big U.S. firms have courses to train men for management.

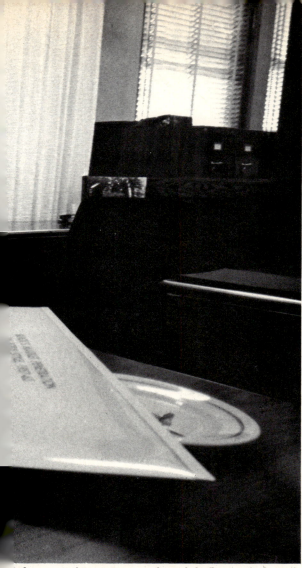

afternoon in his spacious, wood-paneled office in Flint, Mich.

MAN IN A HURRY, Wesley R. Brush, a top automotive marketing executive is a fast-rising member of a highly trained managerial elite

HOME LIFE for Brush centers around his family's large Georgian colonial house in Grand Blanc, a suburb of Flint, where he takes care of one of his daughters while his wife fixes dinner (*above*). Because of Brush's rapid promotions and pay raises, he has moved to larger houses several times since 1950.

SUNDAY DINNER brings the entire family together in a dining alcove off the kitchen (*above*). The Brushes have seven children—five girls and two boys.

FAMILY ENTERTAINMENT before bed is provided by Brush with a duck call (*below*). Despite a heavy schedule, Brush saves some time for his family.

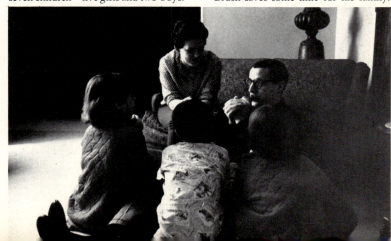

WORKING ON FINAL ASSEMBLY, Lloyd Wells hauls his toolbox past Boeing 727 jet airliners *(above)* parked on "the ramp," an area outside Boeing's large plant in Renton, Wash.

CHECKING A WING FLAP on a 727, Wells works in a big assembly building *(right)*. Known as a top mechanic, Wells was a Boeing "Man of the Month" for an idea he submitted.

VISITING THE UNION, Wells pauses beneath a Lincoln quotation. A member of the International Association of Machinists, he is a union "lead man" and helps supervise work crews.

BARBECUING CHICKENS, Wells entrances his daughter Tamera at a picnic he and his wife gave for their neighbors in the back yard of their pleasant new home in Tacoma.

A MODERN FARMER, H. J. "Jack" Barr
runs a big, mechanized farm and
also serves as a banker and state senator

ON HORSEBACK, Barr amuses his wife and four children by going on a mock roundup. In addition to its cornfields and cattle, Barr's farm produces sugar beets, wheat and feed crops.

IN A CATTLE PEN, Barr *(above, left)* and his younger brother William talk over the progress of steers being fattened for market. The Barr farm covers 6,000 acres near Leoti, Kans.

IN A VAST CORNFIELD, Barr *(far right)* discusses how best to schedule the use of the farm's big planting machines with his brother Kenneth. They talk across the back of Barr's light plane.

IN HIS BANK OFFICE, Barr transacts business by telephone in an informal Western fashion. Board chairman of the First State Bank of Leoti, Barr also serves in the Kansas senate.

AT THE DINNER TABLE in his ranch-style home, Barr is interrupted by a business call from Dallas. Barr is one of many successful men who have turned farming into big business.

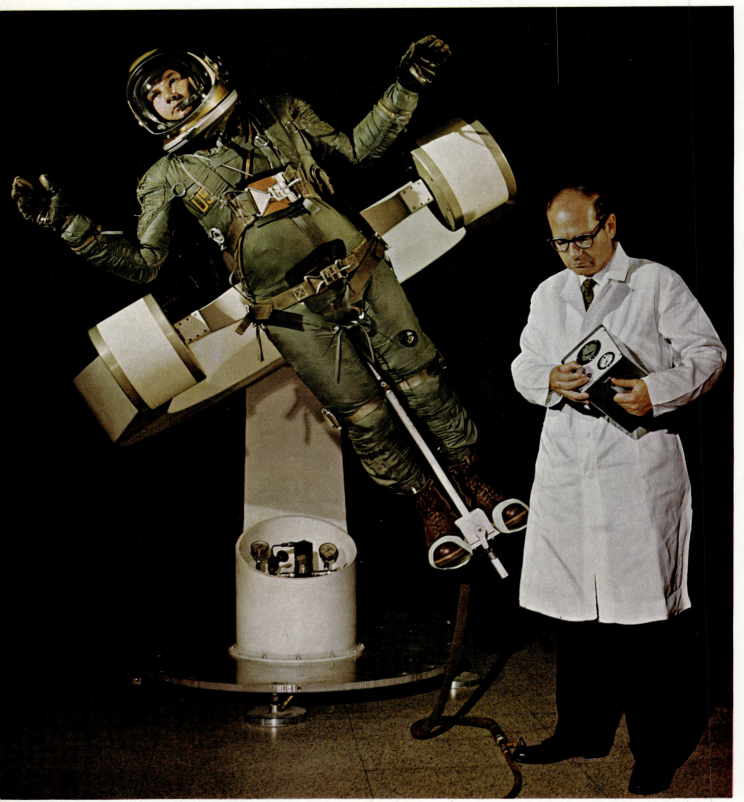

A PRACTICAL EXPERIMENTER, Dr. Fogel is aided by an experimental subject in probing problems of weightlessness in space at the Convair Division of General Dynamics in San Diego, where he is a senior staff scientist. Dr. Fogel has also worked for the National Science Foundation, prepared a report to Congress on scientific costs, and published books.

A JAZZ ENTHUSIAST, Dr. Fogel *(above, with clarinet)* joins four fellow amateur musicians to form a group they call the "Ivory Tower Five." Dr. Fogel is married and has one son.

A CREATIVE THINKER, Dr. Fogel uses a computer to simulate the evolutionary process. He has pioneered in this way of making computers solve difficult mathematical problems.

5

Forging a Nation's Soul and Conscience

by SIGMUND SKARD

THE emergence in the 20th Century of the United States as a world power, simultaneously in politics, economics, the arts and culture, is one of the marvels of modern times. And the chapter on imaginative writing—perhaps the most central of the arts—is not the least surprising part of the story.

But the literary contribution of a people includes not just its authors of world fame. *They* grow from the soil of a more comprehensive tradition wherein the experience of a nation, its needs and its hopes are reflected and embodied in artistic symbols. In the United States this tradition has been elusive. In the words of Henry James, it appears "in too many lights." It is staccato and paradoxical, a history of wasted beginnings, oblivion and rediscovery. It has to be explained on its own terms.

When the handful of British settlers landed on the American East Coast soon after the year 1600 (about half of them to perish from disease and famine during the first winter), it certainly was far from their minds to establish anything like a nation, let alone a national literature. But even in the fields of the arts and writing fate had a future in store for them beyond their wildest imagination.

In their temporary shelter between mountains and sea the Americans were allowed to develop a vigorous self-reliance long denied to other British colonies. Telescoping the growth of centuries, they fast created all the instruments of intellectual life: schools, printing shops and bookstores, libraries, clubs and public press. By the year 1700 Boston was second only to London within the British realm as a center of books. And out of their situation grew even such dreams as literatures are made of.

There was in the first Americans a somber sense of religious destiny, based on few illusions about human nature. But in a way unparalleled in other nations this attitude was married young to the optimistic ideas of rationalist enlightenment. On the virgin soil of the Western continent men of sense and good will were going to establish the ideal home of human liberty and dignity. This grandiose myth of national vocation was fruitful with human tensions. The Americans took up their life in a new land of magnificent beauty and terrifying loneliness. It gave a special meaning to ideas like God and Nature, Man and Society, Past and Present. Their country not only was the promised Eden but concealed an enormous potential wealth, challenging the powers of evil no less than of good. In their isolation the Americans felt the problems of human existence with an immediacy that often made the settlers' professional optimism a whistling in the dark. They were bound for a life of contrasts, with no authority to choose for them. And it was in their Puritan blood to take the choice seriously.

Their problem of identity had its special note, because they belonged to two worlds. Europe was as much a part of American tradition as was America itself, a complicated relationship that long gave the American quest for self-realization a note of uncertainty, at the same time nostalgic and defiant.

But these were only the materials of a national literature: there was no nation as yet. Literary traditions were wholly British. Much of the best of colonial writing was not even printed. The real American contributions before 1776 were institutions and ideas. Men of faith and action dominated the scene, as their portraits dominated contemporary art. They even dominated writing. The theologian Jonathan Edwards' mystic idealism fought his tragic despair; Thomas Jefferson's lofty democratic pathos was balanced by Benjamin Franklin's folksy realism in ways

that would establish traditions. But poetry and literary prose were imitative, with little of distinctive flavor.

There were two exceptions, a symbolic pair. The Puritan Edward Taylor learned from the British "metaphysical" poets to let spirit soar from homeliness. The revolutionary firebrand Philip Freneau made the language of early British Romanticism ring with a slender American note. But the two left no heritage. They opened the line of the forgotten: recognition of their importance did not come until after 1900.

IN the new American state everything was going to be different. There are few parallels in history to the optimism of the young nation, rising like an arc of hope from the Declaration of Independence to the gun reports at Fort Sumter.

Behind its safe walls the United States opened its gates to an increasing flood of immigrants from oppressed Europe. The country was doubling its population every 25 years. And the new American citizens were not just given free soil; they were invited to the millennial Garden of the World. The West had a mystical significance: there nature was creating a new man, Adamic in his innocence. He left behind the memories of declining Europe and gave history a second chance. The first national school of American painting made such dreams come true to the eye, whether they pictured victorious pioneers crossing the Cumberland Mountains or trappers' boats gliding mysteriously through the mists of the Missouri.

But these were the glittering banners of ideals. Within the marching armies beneath them there was already a confusing diversity of conflict. Old regional tensions were given new edge by the motley crowd of immigrants. Old standards were challenged by the newcomers' grassroots democracy and frank materialism. The social picture was changing fast, with rising commercialism and city life; Chicago had 350 inhabitants in 1833 and 300,000 in 1870. And the westward push warned of even more changes to come. The nation was "growing too fast for its virtue and its

SIGMUND SKARD is one of Europe's foremost authorities on U.S. literature. Born in 1903 in Kristiansand, Norway, he took his doctorate at the University of Oslo in 1938. For two years during World War II he was a Consultant to the Library of Congress in Washington and then worked for the U.S. Office of War Information. Since 1946 he has been Professor of Literature, especially American, at Oslo. His books include *The Study of American Literature* (1948) and *The American Myth and the European Mind* (1960).

peace" (Emerson). It needed interpreters of its life more penetrating than the genre painters: a national literature, which read the meanings of the new American realities to the American common man. But this order could not be filled as yet.

Even before the Civil War the changes were too rapid and close, and the aims of the nation too divided. The Americans tried to build their house in the middle of a landslide, and the governing classes on the Eastern seaboard naturally clung to stability, in literature no less than in politics. Their Americanness was only a minor addition to their British culture. And the genteel caution of the literati was little disturbed by more violent influences from abroad. European Romanticism was tamed in democratic America by the survival of rationalist thought, Christian morals and classicist ideals of style. These writers' timidity in handling national characteristics was demonstrated by Washington Irving, an elegant writer whose Americanism was little but a local *piquanterie*.

In the continuation the picture had more shades. Poets like William Cullen Bryant and John Greenleaf Whittier were of harder wood, with a surer grasp of the life around them. There was an early mapping of local and lowly mores, particularly in the South. But all these writers moved within the same peaceful and somewhat tepid atmosphere, and in particular this was the case with the Boston professors and poets who were to set the standards of American literary life almost to the end of the century. They had lofty cultural aims; they were active critics and competent writers. Many of the textbook heroes of the Americans were created by them. But the nation they knew was limited, and their image of it, even in Longfellow, was made to fit a fading European taste.

THUS it was left to a group of outsiders, less respectable and less conventional, to answer the more vigorous urges of Romanticism and to delve into wider and deeper layers of American life.

Surprisingly, the real beginning was made by the gentleman novelist James Fenimore Cooper. He knew little about Romantic philosophy. But his boyish delight in life and his sweeping power of narration opened new fields to American literature: recent history, the sea, the primeval forest. The romantic dream of the wilderness even added freshness and beauty to his stilted style. Against that background appeared Leatherstocking, the great mythical figure of the free American, legitimate son of unspoiled nature and decent society. And there was more to Cooper: his innate conservatism made him see and describe even the depravity fostered by the wilderness, and the threatening signs of decay within established society. His world fame was based on American realities. He is the literary overture to the century.

The door that Cooper left only ajar was thrown wide open by Ralph Waldo Emerson. His Transcendentalism was no dusty philosophy. What gathered a group of starry-eyed youngsters around him in the New England of the 1830s was his exultant call for fresh beginnings, voiced with the clarity of a silver horn. Christian ideas were at the foundation of Emerson's thought. But he merged them painlessly with Franklin's good sense, the Romantic individualism and mysticism of his foreign masters, and the pioneer spirit of the Western frontier: alone should man face his open universe, untrammeled by the past, guided by God through benevolent nature, in that land where man finally had been allowed to mold his own fate. And Emerson drew the everyday conclusions with surprising acumen, in an abrupt prose where glittering ideas sprang symbolically from hard, clear Yankee images. To him, life was a continuous experiment. So were his own poems, which talked stumblingly to the world in a new, American voice.

NOT all human facts of the time would yield to this interpretation, however. Even Emerson's friends sometimes felt annoyed by his paradoxes and by his cheerful acceptance of himself, the world and even "the dear old devil." There is a significant shade of difference already in his most faithful disciple, Henry David Thoreau. In Thoreau's single important book, describing his lonely sojourn at Walden Pond, there is a muscular toughness of style, a willful and biting wit, and a sense of the primitive undercurrent of wildness in life that goes beyond his master and feels like a corrective. After 1850, when the sky darkened with the gathering clouds of the Civil War, Emerson's Americanism appeared as too shallow, and to nobody more than to Nathaniel Hawthorne.

The two were neighbors in peaceful Concord, but in mind there was an abyss between them. Hawthorne was a skeptic toward everything. His thought was permeated by the Puritan sense of guilt. All his writing circles around the nature of sin, above all in that isolated individual who was so glorified by the

Transcendentalists. Hawthorne's real field was the middle ground between reality and allegory, and he found it most easily in the past, which to him was an inescapable part of the present. In *The Scarlet Letter* he created the first great American psychological and historical novel, national even in its ideas. Hawthorne's Adam and Eve have little innocence left, and their only hope is learning from their fall. Such was Hawthorne's lesson to his adolescent nation.

Herman Melville found his battleground even farther away. Much more than Hawthorne he knew from experience the cruelty of life. This insight strengthened his pity for his fellow beings, suspended in a world that to him was formed not in Emersonian love but in inscrutable malice. In a series of books moving within fictional or artificially isolated milieus Melville traced the ill fate of man and his dreams at the hands of unknown gods. And in *Moby-Dick* he gave majestic expression to the torment of his thought: the grippingly realistic account of a whaling expedition, where spirit and blubber grotesquely fuse, and the breathless hunt actually goes for the Riddle of Life itself. All the elemental metaphysical problems are raised, in a crescendo of despair, within the heaving walls of the little whaling vessel, which symbolizes both democratic America and cosmic Earth.

Natty Bumppo

Edgar Allan Poe had to escape from everyday reality altogether in order to look through it. In his poems and short stories he created a world within his own mind, a phantasmagoric scene curiously logical in its details, where he could stage his distorted visions of perversion and morbidity, only relieved momentarily by glimpses of bodiless beauty. Even more than Hawthorne and Melville, Poe was a lonely delver into the depths of the mind, a symbolist in principle, tied to expanding contemporary America largely by his negation of its dominant values.

To bring such contrasts together in any kind of synthesis must seem impossible. But Walt Whitman managed. He was spiritually baptized by Emerson and his faith in self-reliant man. But Whitman was as carnal and expansive as Emerson was bookish and reserved. The "self" that boisterously yawped in Whitman's first poems was a representative man. In his *Leaves of Grass* the poet reflected in his own "body electric" all of America—the frontier West, the seaboard, the cities—with its range of human life, its greatness and misery, embracing its conflicting elements in an immense gesture of identification.

If this love en masse did not appear ridiculous (or only rarely so), it was because of Whitman's spontaneous warmth toward all forms of existence, his original and redeeming naïveté, and, with growing age, his deepened humility toward loneliness, suffering and death, in himself and in his fellow beings. His optimism was seared by sorrow. And he swept his readers off their feet by an irresistible poetic suggestiveness that created its own supple form and sometimes even pointed toward the surrealism of the future. He ridiculed the correct versifiers of his day. What he envisaged was a literature that merged Romantic emotion and stark, modern realities in the service of a new culture, national in a deeper sense.

But his work was just a beginning, as was that of his great contemporaries. There was no real milieu around them; they certainly were not regarded as the core of contemporary writing. In the words of T. S. Eliot, "it is only in retrospect that their Americanness is fully visible." Cooper soon was reduced to the status of a children's writer. Hawthorne's fame remained limited, Poe's even more so; Thoreau was overlooked, Whitman condemned and Melville completely forgotten. Emerson was treated with increasing respect, but not always for the best reasons; and if his books sold by the hundreds, those of Longfellow sold by the thousands.

IN the period following the Civil War there hardly seemed to be room for any tradition at all. During the five decades down to 1914 the landslide turned into an avalanche. Agrarian expansion was followed by an equally sudden development of industry and finance, supported by a new flood of immigrants even more heterogeneous than before. By 1920 only 41 per cent of the U.S. population was of British stock. In these new masses a new type of civilization sprang up with unheard-of violence, marked by urbanization, big money, economic exploitation, bitter social struggle and a brutal worship of material values. Pioneer hopefulness reappeared as a vulgar social Darwinism, barely disguised by Transcendentalist phrases about the grandeur of the individual.

But through this apparent chaos a new pattern was already emerging—modern, continental America as we know it, with new foundations for unity. Toward the end of the period, immigration came virtually to an end; the settlement was over. The new transport system, the new economic organization and the developing means of mass communication increasingly wiped out regional differences, but at the same time created the possibility of a deeper national coalescence. New tools of scholarly life originated in the reorganized universities, which made world contributions to research even before 1900. The study of American intellectual and literary history began in earnest. In pessimist Henry Adams the country had its first great philosopher of civilization.

In facing this new world American imaginative writing worked under severe handicaps. The Boston school, and its even more colorless successors, still represented the "official" face of literature. Before the end of the century the great American writers were rarely studied even in American colleges. On a lower level, writing was dominated by a sub-literature that offered an easy escape from a complicated existence.

BUT there were more promising signs. The new American life itself created demands for a new American literature. These demands sprang from immediate and overwhelming facts: a new existence, which faced the population with countless human problems. Behind such demands there was also a groping urge, radical or Christian or both, to reestablish the American dream of human happiness even under the new and less favorable conditions.

This literary movement toward "realism" of some kind or other had one of its roots in American soil, in a folksy, humorous storytelling that was not always fit for delicate ears. The new literature originated spontaneously in widely scattered regions. Some of these books were sentimentally nostalgic, but others showed a fine grasp of problems, psychology and style. They began building a new, mutual understanding in the nation. And they were placed in a larger context by William Dean Howells, who justly saw this "Local Color School" as an extension of the European movement of Realism. His

own excellent novels and his broadminded work as a critic meant the beginning of the end of the Boston predominance. He was gradually surrounded by an increasing number of good Realistic novelists who faced American life and its problems more and more undauntedly, often with a strong social pathos.

Notwithstanding, there was a caution even in Howells. He believed in the old virtues and in their power to prevail in the face of brutal forces. A younger generation of writers made those forces their real subject. They were Naturalists in the sense of their European masters, adopting the Europeans' social determinism together with their literary technique. That attitude ran too heavily against the "bright" American tradition to be accepted. Even Realism came late to the States; Naturalism was delayed by several decades. The books of the first Naturalists were either suppressed (as happened to Theodore Dreiser) or quietly ignored.

Hester Prynne

But there was more to this delay than external pressure: an uncertainty in the writers themselves. Beside the willingness to describe life as it was ran an equally strong and equally American urge to see life as it should have been, transformed by ideas or by the free power of art. In some novelists these crossing motives made Naturalism an episode in their career. In others, like Frank Norris, they created a curious mixture of Naturalism and mystic symbolism. There was an anti-Realistic trend in poetry, in the lonely efforts of Sidney Lanier and Edwin Arlington Robinson to give voice to the complexities of modern life within the bonds of literary tradition. The paragon of this multiplicity was Stephen Crane, who made his Naturalistic material serve an almost Freudian depth psychology and in his style moved into Impressionism and beyond.

The two overpowering talents of the period both followed the same tortuous roads, giving a deeper sense to "reality."

Emily Dickinson lived as a spinster and recluse in her father's house in Amherst, Massachusetts, devoting her 1,775 poems to the tiny details of an externally eventless life. But her playful Emersonian intellectuality was deceptive: hers was a modern mind. She looked at her own puppet world with an eye as coolly analytical as that of any social novelist. Her lifelong conversation with God and herself (no other audience attending at the time) is the ruthless dissection of a soul, mingling skeptic wit, flippant morbidity and wild despair with dazzling visions of heaven. Her anonymous life gained cosmic dimension through an elemental symbolic power growing out of things small and near in the old American tradition.

HENRY JAMES seemed to differ from Emily Dickinson as widely as humanly possible, but only apparently so. He was a man of the world, an early advocate of Realism in Howells' sense. But he soon left America with its "silent past and deafening present." He moved to England, physically and spiritually, and concentrated his literary analysis on the decrepit upper classes of society from both sides of the ocean, a self-created and partly artificial milieu where James could study in laboratory isolation those basic powers of the individual soul that became his all-absorbing interest, most frequently in a confrontation of New World innocence with Old World sophistication and decay. An increasing pedantry of analysis and involution of style made James's later novels inaccessible to the multitude. After his period of oblivion they were to become the sacred books of fictional technique, vying with Hawthorne's in their moral perceptiveness, their subdued and terrifying power of emotion, and their deep understanding of the American mind seen from a vantage point outside America.

That kind of vantage point was sadly denied to the mysterious stranger of the period, Mark Twain. Twain had absorbed the new continental America more completely even than Whitman. And from the popular tall-talers he had acquired the art of bringing anything across to an audience, by mouth or pen, with flashing lucidity. He was more than a spinner of yarns; he had the sensitivity of a child, lofty ideals in the great American tradition and emotional depth. But he never lived up to his scattered promises. His life and times were too complicated and left him confused. He spellbound the world with a burlesque humor that revolutionized American

prose by its direct simplicity but left little in memory when laughter died away. In a serious vein he moved with occasional brilliance from bitter realism to sheer romance. But his thought was a muddle and his grasp often uncertain. With advancing age he came to hate both mankind and himself. Only when he moved back into his own past, a childhood America before the flood, were dreams and reality, humor and tragedy reconciled in moving symbols of cruelty and kindness, innocence and death. The puzzled world insisted on seeing Twain largely as a humorist and author of juveniles. He is no less puzzling as we see him now.

Huckleberry Finn

No clear, definite pattern emerges from these contrasts. But the variegation is fruitful. The pictorial arts of the time show the same groping quest: domination by wizened Academism with its hodgepodge of borrowed styles, an acceptable American Realism in the placid landscapes of George Inness and the dramatic canvases of Winslow Homer, an unacceptable Naturalism in Thomas Eakins (forgotten until after his death in 1916), a refinement of artistry in the expatriates James Abbott McNeill Whistler and John Singer Sargent—and then, as widely separated as two poles, Albert Pinkham Ryder's somber Melvillian passion and Louis Sullivan's first skyscraper. But as in literature it was a confusion of promise, not of despair.

THE sudden gathering of these forces into that flowering of American cultural life that fills the span of years between the two World Wars is a phenomenon that nobody can explain. The birth of talent is always a mystery. But there are facts to make the possibilities understandable.

That political and social consolidation which had begun before 1914 continued all through the period. So did nationwide economic expansion and ethnic integration, at least of the noncolored groups. War and Depression were national experiences; so was recovery under the New Deal, with its plans and its atmosphere of hope. There was the unifying impact of radio, the movies and the automobile, the explosive development of higher education, the growth of new intellectual milieus, the influence of foreign thought from Freud to Marx and general changes in American mores. Significant was the growth in scholarship. The United States won its first Nobel Prize for research in 1907; by 1945 there were 16 more. And the expansion was not only in medicine, technology and science but also in political and social sciences, including fields like psychology and history.

The arts shared in this development. Jazz had its breakthrough in and outside America after World War I, and it was only one part of a new creativity in American music. New forms of popular art developed, such as musical comedy. America continued to make its original contribution to modern architecture. In the pictorial arts the experimental school of "The Eight," together with the Armory Show of 1913, brought American art into the modern mainstream, with group contributions like the social and the American scene schools, and with a long line of individual artists as diverse as Charles Sheeler and Edward Hopper, Ben Shahn and Georgia O'Keeffe. But above all it was literature that now showed the visage of America to the world.

IN new forums of debate—universities, theaters, periodicals, books—literature was made a matter of concern to the nation by a young and brilliant generation of critics. Whether they were liberal or radical, moralist or Bohemian, "neohumanist" or "Southern agrarian," they all asked for writing that could again become a molding force in human life.

Parallel to this program for the future ran the search for a usable past, which helped create a new understanding of the values of American literary tradition. The "American mind" in the broadest sense became a subject of research. This work found its focus in the journal *American Literature* (from 1929), its organization in the American Studies movement, and in 1948 reached its first great goal in the cooperative *Literary History of the United States*. One of the results was an amazing series of rereadings, or rebirths, of older American authors.

The creative literature that grew from this new soil was baffling in its richness and diversity. One result of this expansion was a growing sense of literary self-reliance. Many members of the young generation were expatriates and hated America, at least for a time. But they themselves belonged to an American tradition nevertheless, sometimes without knowing it.

One striking aspect was their inclusive choice of material. Historical subjects played no central part except in disguised forms. But the first great novels about the settlement of the prairies came now, as did the first great poems about the conquistadors and about the Civil War. Much stronger was the regional trend, until American literature covered practically all sections of New America, city and countryside.

EVEN more striking was the broad range of ideas. For the first time in history imaginative writing in America offered the widest panorama of what was happening in the national mind. Literary art reflected the graphic curve of tradition and revolt, despondency and hope, from the jazz age in the 1920s to the new confidence in the following decade. There was a variety of attitudes among the writers toward their own country, covering the full spectrum from abhorrence to devotion and all the shades in between.

The same catholicity characterized technique. Beside the final breakthrough of Naturalism there was a fresh experimentation in poetry, prose and playwriting, closely tied to new subjects and with no inhibitions toward using the juicy American idiom. There was a new eclecticism of form, choosing or blending literary methods according to the immediate aim. This creativity, springing from urgent national needs, also gained a new relevance to mankind, as, from World War I on, the differences between the United States and the Old World were gradually diminishing. The six literary Nobel Prizes granted to Americans so far are a symbol of this general equalization of standards.

In sorting this vast array of authors genre by genre the critics by now have everybody placed according to this or that criterion, as neatly as the angels in Dante's Paradise. Within our narrow space it is more appropriate to delight irresponsibly in the gay motleyness of form and color in this new Garden of the World and its tropic lack of regimentation.

In European poetry of the interwar years the overpowering figure was American-born T. S. Eliot. The major part of his own writing and criticism rightly belongs to Great Britain, and the impact of his work, of course, was due to the depth and honesty of his poetic message. But his background was American, as was his early work; and in the international revolution of poetic technique inaugurated by Eliot there were strong American elements, not least in the return to a spoken language swept clean of clichés. Second to the master in importance was Ezra Pound, also an American expatriate, inspirational both by his restless hunger for novelty and by his ponderous and private erudition.

But the American "modernism" that followed in the footsteps of these founding fathers is much too multicolored to be called a school. It ranges from the regional group of Southern poets to the timeless microstudies of Marianne Moore and the electric display of e. e. cummings; and their inventions mingled happily in an amazing concourse of other forces and tendencies, aims and objects. There seem to be astronomic distances between Hart Crane's Icarian attempt to create a national myth and William Carlos Williams' caustic vignettes of life in small-town America, or between Vachel Lindsay's drumming rhythms and Elinor Wylie's ring of hard brilliance. But they all belong together, building and adding variety to that unity of which they form a part.

Two poets are classics already, Robert Frost and Wallace Stevens—who are different in practically all respects. Frost is the genial and majestic spokesman of old, rural America, turning its "simple" forms of existence into symbols, speaking in Franklin's voice about Melville's problems, with a note that is curiously recognizable even to average modern Americans who hardly ever see a living cow. Stevens is the poet of the abstract and impersonal modern world, disguising and rearranging it willfully in endless artistic refinement, "resisting the intelligence almost successfully" and speaking in many voices, strange to everybody and sometimes even to himself. But at bottom the two poets are brothers of the spirit, asking with sly earnest that same tough question and answering it from their different materials: how is modern man able to exist within that frail and transient world he has to create for himself alone?

EVEN more confusing is the galaxy of interwar novelists. These authors faced most directly the unbelievable changes of the world in the 1920s and 1930s. And in all its phases the confrontation created great art.

The somber note was struck by the Naturalists, like Sherwood Anderson and James T. Farrell, with their deadening documentation of suffering and human waste. No relief was to be had from F. Scott Fitzgerald's symbolic figures of the flapper age and Erskine Caldwell's grotesques from Southern rural decay. Even in the less sensational work of Willa Cather and the other "women novelists" there is a sense of flight from a world that is no longer quite understandable.

But in other writers burns a redeeming fire of hope. In his tragic panorama of the U.S.A. John Dos Passos also included glimpses of that traditional "American Dream." Sinclair Lewis' scathing satire was softened by his sense of genial fellowship with his victims. Thomas Wolfe turned himself into the Whitman-esque symbol of a hard-won reacceptance of America. And John Steinbeck is in the same tradition, uneven and blundering, but always again conquering by the generous warmth of his understanding, since Emerson the strongest spokesman of American affirmation.

THREE novelists are on a level of their own. Theodore Dreiser came out of the seething jungle of industrialized and metropolitan U.S.A., the first outstanding American writer with a non-British name. The foundation of his work was his personal experience. His books are clumsy repetitions of the same depressing facts, often amassed with a patience larger than that of his readers. But by curious contradiction it is this artless technique that makes Dreiser a great writer. His books are not literary interpretations; they are slices of life itself. He allows life to ask its own questions, and the effect is overwhelming.

Ernest Hemingway played a different instrument. He came out of the tritest Middle West and left America happily, spending most of his life in exotic places, describing war and love, hunting and bullfighting and other manly pursuits in a blunt and tight-lipped style that made him the hero of several "lost generations." Only gradually was it discovered that Hemingway the writer had little to do with the legend about the man, that he was an artist hunting frantically for new dimensions, that his spare language teems with double meanings, and that his seemingly calloused and obtuse characters represent romantic and tragic attitudes toward life. "One must be narrow to penetrate," said Henry James; Hemingway is a case in point.

The third star burned with the brightest but also the most flickering flame. William Faulkner came from the South and never actually left it. His immense lifework was the patient construction of a Southern realm of imagination, as real and unreal as that of Poe, and peopled no less with horror and violence. In the beginning Faulkner's literary nightmares were regarded with disgust, as were the subtleties of his technique. But postwar Europe discovered the deeper import of his creation: a harrowing poetic legend of man's condition, his degradation and corruption, under the modern breakdown of traditional values, subtly supported by Faulkner's artistic innovations. His work is Southern in its ideas and form but not in its relevance. His cosmic pessimism is matched by a universal sense of human dignity: hope against hope is his message to our time. With him the "dark" tradition in American literature became a world power.

The real epitome of these contrasts is the father of American drama, Eugene O'Neill.

Theater is old in the United States, and O'Neill had it in his blood. But he was the first American to make the stage a mirror of the deepest conflicts of his time. He had the most motley human background, around and in himself, and his religious tradition forced him again and again to probe his material for the deepest verities. In his huge production he turned to the most diverse times, milieus and human fates and handled them with a chameleonic versatility of technique. But his main subject is the metaphysical predicament of man, discussed in a seemingly planless vacillation between hope and despair.

O'Neill is jerky even as a craftsman; his language may be banal, his shiftiness tiring. But his impact on his time has been immense, both on modern theater generally and especially on the American stage, which in effect he created and which became a living force in his own lifetime. The searching seriousness of conviction in his best work makes him one of the most meaningful figures of a great period.

BUT this precarious balance did not last long. World War II was a much more traumatic experience for Americans than was the 1914-1918 conflict: so much more was involved. The war ended on a note of hope. But the new world proved to be one that had not been foreseen.

Decisive was a new internal transformation of the United States itself; the ground was moving again. The "open" American society was gradually closing under the impact of a new coordination and organization of power, discreet and inexorable, in all walks of life. The old "people" was swiftly disappearing, together with old classes, standards and distinctions, leaving the individual isolated in the mass, powerless, passive and anonymous. "Causes" and "ideals" were evaporating; the machinery of society was becoming too complicated for understanding. Even personal conflicts seemed to be losing their edge, leveled under the impact of short-range comfort, manufactured mores and opinions, and synthetic happiness.

This description may be a rough sketch more than a map. But the tendencies doubtless were there. In his world of enameled efficiency the new American man was subjected to new pressures, internal and external. His seemingly well-adjusted existence was often marred by anxiety, confusion and frustration. And the larger world, terrorized by the Cold War, missiles and The Bomb, offered little relief. Everywhere the same transformation was under way, in forms that made old differences obsolete. Cherished American characteristics lost their meaning on a globe where "materialism" reigned supreme, where in all languages "innocence" was a word only of the dictionary, where the "power of blackness" was visible to the naked eye and the hopeful feeling of fresh beginnings was rare indeed, except perhaps among the Astronauts.

THE "Europe complex" of the Americans faded away in this process, together with Old Europe itself. Much more frankly than before they now accepted their Americanness as a part of the human fate. But there was little exultation about it. The American cultural contribution, in scholarship and international discussion, pop culture and the arts, was more and more taken as a matter of course, in a world where distances hardly existed any more and English was the common language. The paintings of Andrew Wyeth and Jackson Pollock were now accepted no less cordially in Berlin than in Boston. But they hardly carried much of a "message to the world," and often it was difficult to say what was "American" about them.

In these new surroundings even American literature faced strange tasks and difficulties.

There were obstacles of an external kind. Serious literature came under increasing pressure from the new mass media. If the pocket book had its redeeming qualities, the same could not be said about much of press, radio and television, and the bulk of printed entertainment. The ever-increasing time for leisure was of dubious benefit to literature in a society where all living rooms had become movie theaters with continuous programs and where language itself was wearing down under the impact of technology and advertising.

In reaction, literature isolated itself. Increasingly, literary taste and judgment found their real strongholds in the universities. The New Criticism has been called the most significant American intellectual contribution of the period. But with age the movement tended to congeal into radical conventionalism and critical fashion, creating a uniformity in reverse. Many writers were just writing for each other; they saw no hope that literature could ever again become a power in society.

There may also have been an exhaustion in the writers themselves, which was noticeable not in the United States alone. There was, and still is, a good deal of experimentation with form, not least in the theater. But there is not the old excitement about it; sources are drying up, and absurdity has its own limits. Even in the interwar years the author often had to admit that he lived in a desperate world. But there was still a common ground of understanding: forms of social organization, standards of behavior, moral and metaphysical assumptions that were tacitly accepted. Literature was concerned with man's place within this established world, even if he revolted against it. Now the individual has fewer traditional props to support him. To many human beings God has disappeared from life together with nature, morality is fleetingly relative, society itself vague and yet unassailable. Like his forefathers, the American has to find and maintain his own self, stumbling through an unknown wilderness. But instead of palpable dangers he faces little formless fears, and no longer does he feel around him the warm company of fellow beings. Even for literature this is a difficult proposition.

MANY writers do not share this plight of their subjects: they have their own ground to stand on. American traditional values were not eradicated during the years 1939 to 1945, nor have they been since. Even in the sneering literature that came out of the war itself affirmation of an American heritage could be found. And it became stronger and more verbal in the following decades. There remains a struggling liberal tradition, with a lineage dating back to the American Revolution. Sometimes it is also linked to a new cultural nationalism.

However, these ideas have not proved very fruitful as a stimulant of literary creation. This is not the time for the great historical, political or social novel of the old type, nor for the patriotic hymn. American democracy today seems to have little more inspirational value to writers than has the idea of America's mission in the world. And the same holds true of political conservatism. The honest and service-minded businessman apparently has no future as a literary hero.

DIFFERENT is that traditionalism which grows from a deeper soil. Since the 1920s such ideas have had their center in the South. More or less explicitly the writers of the "Southern Renaissance" dissociate themselves from the liberal interpretation of American history. Against modern democratic society, with its rationalism and individualism and its acquisitive technical civilization, the Southern writers raise up the social and moral values of a living past, harking back to the standards of the organic class society that was destroyed by the frontier and the Civil War.

This literature draws its real strength not from political and social utopias but from a feeling of fellowship and shared ideals in a region and a human group. There is a similar quest for roots and heritage in other groups, such as the Jews—although their background is completely urban—and the Negroes, with their violent additional note of social protest.

How long such cultural enclaves will survive, however, nobody knows. In any case, many authors of the postwar years feel no such adherence. They are disaffiliated from society, its groupings and standards in an alienation more complete than would have been thinkable a few decades ago. In the great nation of joiners, loneliness of the soul has become the basic problem.

Few of these writers feel their isolation to be a happy wall around their personal lives; most of them face their situation with despair. And the problem limits their vision. As a refuge from the anonymous pressure of society they focus their interest frantically on those few fields of human activity where there is still some liberty of action—the exotic, esoteric, neurotic, the life of the child and sex. Their books picture a fragmented world of grotesques, dominated by an evil described for its own sake, without religious connotation. The writer is involved in an endless play with ironies and ambiguities, sometimes presented with whimpering self-pity.

But this is only one group. In others, tragedy certainly is there. But it is the result of an honest quest for self-knowledge under deadening conditions, a longing for some kind of love and contact, a fight for human dignity and personal freedom. And the effort itself carries a value, even if it is thwarted and frustrated. The attempt to be true to oneself implies a moral standard of consistency and responsibility. In many of these books the positive residue is minimal. In Sartre's words, for the writer it is "not a matter of believing in man, but of wanting to." Nevertheless, this hesitant affirmation shows that even on its most barren ground recent American literature is not completely void of hope.

Neither is it wholly suspended in the air. The necessity of choice in a world of polarities is no new situation to the American writer. In spite of its immediate alienation the new generation of authors solidly belongs to a tradition, claiming the heritage of Faulkner and James, Melville and Poe, Hawthorne and the old Puritans as strongly as it rejects the other, "brighter" line.

WHETHER, 30 years from now, these writers will arrange themselves in a literary hierarchy, dominated by, say, Robert Lowell and Theodore Roethke, Arthur Miller and Tennessee Williams, Saul Bellow, Ralph Ellison and Robert Penn Warren, as neatly as the interwar literature now circles under its zodiac, nobody knows today. (When speaking of American literature one also has to reserve several seats for baffling rediscoveries.) Even less do we know how balanced their picture of the United States will appear to be by then. In any case, whatever the answer to such questions turns out to be, the writing of these Americans, and of many more, certainly matches any other great national literature of our time.

But its impact is difficult to judge. Within a world community sighing under the burden of Existentialist thought, American writers today speak an international language even more than they did in the 1920s and 1930s. But there is no sign as yet that

their work has brought to their contemporaries that revelation of unsounded depths that came from their predecessors 40 years ago.

Thus, this sketch of American literature does not end on an optimistic note. But it is not an optimistic literature.

AMERICAN history began with a dream, and in many ways this dream materialized. Hardly any other nation has been able, through the centuries, to offer personal liberty and the elementary conditions of happiness to so great a part of its population. And by their modern leadership in technology the Americans have been instrumental in promoting that development, which now, to an increasing extent, is making such conditions available around the globe.

But from the very beginning there was in the American mind an awareness that life is complicated and serious, that our dreams are frail and often have little correlation to our external well-being. These tensions have offered to American imaginative writing its strongest inspiration. American literary art has flowered not in the sunshine of the "four freedoms" but in their shadow; and more often than not the dialogue has been carried on amid hesitations and doubt. Now the doubters may prove to be right. To the prophets of disaster, that new world of which America is the outstanding example may now be facing the bitter alternative of complete extinction or serfdom under its own civilization.

The future is not decided by writers. And at best the prognosis is uncertain: there is too much we do not know. But it may be safe to say that if the world still has a future, and if, even in the continuation, man's mind is going to be able to influence his fate, American literature can hardly avoid playing its part, as long as it lives up to its own traditions. In its strongest representatives, old and new, there has always been a ruthless, realistic awareness of the human condition. And the more honestly these writers penetrated the depths of their own minds, the more their findings meant to the world.

About 200 years ago J. Hector St. John de Crèvecoeur wrote of America's "close affinity with our present time." Through its disjointed and checkered history American literature repeatedly has proved such words to be true. It may happen again, in the world we are now facing.

FAMED MASTERPIECE by the great American architect Frank Lloyd Wright, a house called "Falling Water" juts out over a waterfall and blends with the Pennsylvania countryside.

STARTLING SKYSCRAPER, the Price Tower in Bartlesville, Okla., is dedicated by Wright *(far right)* in 1956. Wright, who died in 1959, deeply influenced many other architects.

An Explosion of Creativity in the Nation's Art

Even in its raw youth America had a startling number of fine painters and its architecture often had a noble simplicity. In the 20th Century there has been nothing less than an explosion in the arts. Frank Lloyd Wright, brilliant pupil of the pioneering Louis Sullivan, became the country's most daring, and most discussed, architect. Literally dozens of first-rank painters emerged. Some portrayed America with painful realism, breaking utterly with the Romantic school of the 19th Century. Abstract painters broke with the Realists, eventually forming the New York "school" of Abstract Expressionism, for a time the world's most influential art movement. And the U.S. art world remains in bubbling ferment as the schools of "Pop Art," "Op Art" and "Hard-Edge" painting seek ways to render their visions of reality.

OLD MASTER, Alexander Calder, born in 1898, makes sculptures from metal cutouts and wire. His hanging "mobiles" move with a humorous grace; his "stabiles" have massive simplicity.

EARLY DRAWINGS by Calder depicting an acrobat in motion show his lifelong concern "with the way things are hooked together." Another early work was a complex, animated toy circus.

CONTEMPORARY CONGLOMERATION, *Talisman* by Robert Rauschenberg, one of America's leading young artists, incorporates such objects as old photographs and bottles. Winner of several prizes, Rauschenberg is often called a "Pop" artist since he draws on popular culture, but he considers himself a journalist who sees the commonplace from a fresh angle.

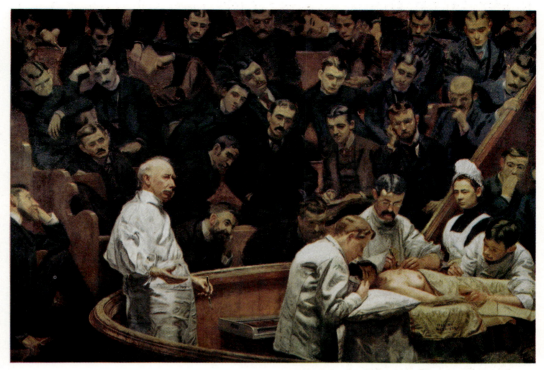

METICULOUS DETAIL in Thomas Eakins' *The Agnew Clinic* reflects the artist's rejection of the conventionally pretty and his mastery of the painter's craft.

LYRIC VISION of Albert Pinkham Ryder's *Moonlight Marine* evokes the sea's brooding mystery. Ryder, a moody recluse, painted scenes from his imagination.

ROUGH EXUBERANCE glows from George Bellows' *Dempsey and Firpo*, a painting of a famous fight. Bellows recorded the seamier side of U.S. life.

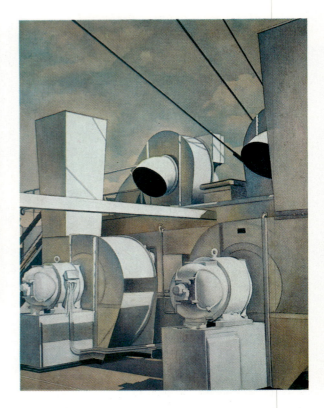

EDWARD HOPPER tries to catch the look and feel of America in such paintings of commonplace scenes as *Chop Suey (above)*. A quiet craftsman, Hopper is a master at painting the effects of light.

CHARLES SHEELER, who died in 1965, rendered harsh, angular, machine-age shapes, such as those in *Upper Deck (right)*, with such near-photographic fidelity that his works almost become abstract designs.

GEORGIA O'KEEFFE, the country's most eminent woman painter,
evokes the vastness of the South-
west's deserts in *Antelope (above)*.
Her paintings are characterized by
clean colors and strong patterns.

BEN SHAHN re-creates himself as
a child watching street musicians
(*left*) in *Portrait of Myself When
Young*, from New York's Museum
of Modern Art. Shahn is known
for his social protest painting.

ANDREW WYETH displays his
remarkable technique in his portrait *Miss Olson (right)*. Often using tempera—an exacting medium
—Wyeth paints scenes around his
homes in Pennsylvania and Maine.

PIONEERS in Abstract painting established the country's position in the vanguard of modern art

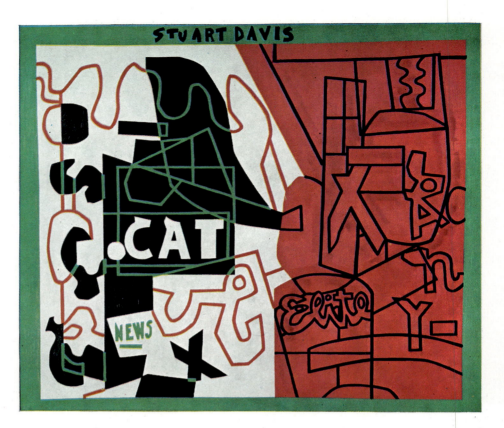

STUART DAVIS

JAZZ RHYTHMS underlie Stuart Davis' brightly colored *Pochade (right)*. Davis, who died in 1964, painted complex but humorous Abstract designs, often punctuated by words and given lively, slangy titles like *The Paris Bit*.

EVOCATIVE PATTERNS of Mark Tobey's *Awakening Night* were inspired by the spectacle of a city's lights coming on. Tobey, who works fast "so as not to lose the rhythmic impulse," was an early leader in Abstractionism.

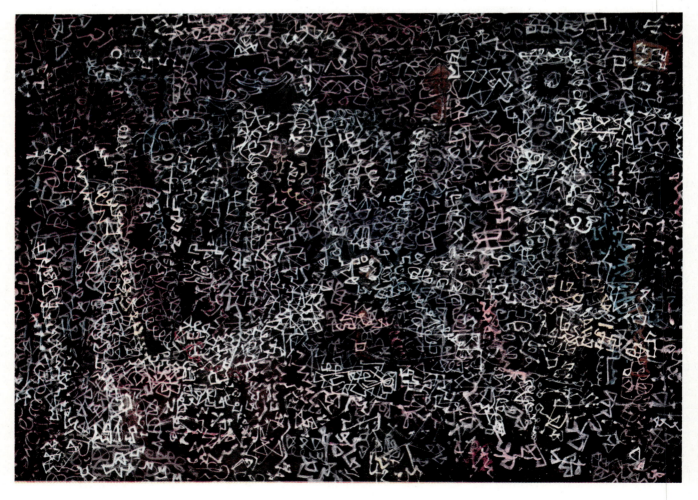

ABSTRACT SEACOAST by the watercolorist John Marin evokes waves breaking on the rocky Maine coast. Marin, who saw nature as geometric forms and tilting planes, delighted in bringing motion and fresh air into his paintings.

PLANNED DISORDER of the swirling patterns in *Convergence (below)* was made by Jackson Pollock, who dripped and smeared paint onto his canvases. Until his death in 1956 Pollock was a leader of Abstract Expressionism.

The Busy Search for Leisure

by PETER VON ZAHN

THERE they come, there they are—on foot, on horseback, in automobiles, in golf carts—hurriedly pressing on toward their long weekend. Over the hills, along the coasts, in the water, on land and in the air they search for leisure. Millions belong to this troop—more than 190 million as a matter of fact, not counting invalids, babies, and a few executives of General Motors who are too busy to have any fun. They stream six abreast through the gates of the football and baseball stadiums. They carry duck guns, baseball bats or canoe paddles on their shoulders; they hold fishing rods and guitars in their hands. Most of them wear sunglasses before their eyes, and many wear diving masks. The transistor radio is seldom missing. Their clothing is of dazzling colors and leaves much brown skin uncovered; this is particularly noticeable among the women.

When the column comes to a halt, photographs are snapped and the portable television sets are turned on so that each can see how the good cowboy brings the outlaw to justice. When they break camp after the pause, oceans of Coca-Cola have been consumed; left behind are towers of trash. As the hamburger stand closes, a policeman clanking with martial metal writes down the name of the little girl who has lost her parents. The masses in their cars see in front of them an infinite chain of cars, in the rearview mirrors more cars; over them flies the helicopter directing traffic on the outskirts of the city. They hear an announcement on the radio that 570 leisure seekers will die in traffic accidents during this long weekend. But they do not think about death. They think about life. Their worries are whether they can still get a reservation in a motel on Route 40 and whether or not the beer in the cooler is still cold.

On the back seats of the cars lie *Mad* magazine, *Holiday*, a half-read copy of *Fanny Hill* and the AAA Triptik with the thick blue line drawn by the young woman at the counter. They move to the South when it gets cold in the North and to the North when the long school vacation begins. They are excited about going West, as if they might discover something left undiscovered by Lewis and Clark. They scatter in the great expanse, but they crowd together by the thousands where a well-known folk singer is performing or where someone in leather chaps is balancing for eight seconds on an unsaddled horse or where a man in a gray uniform and a wide-brimmed slouch hat is re-enacting a long-dead general's heroic ride across a famous battlefield (the man's real job is selling insurance).

These leisure seekers are not afraid of the rain because they have transparent plastic coverings for their hats and coats. They are not afraid of the cold because their cars are well heated. In general, however, they seek the sun—which their ancestors laboring in hot fields cursed. Many even seek solitude. But this is not always easy to find—except perhaps on the rocking chairs and porches of old wooden houses in villages that the troops of millions shun.

Always new troops; always new camp followers and marauders; the procession never comes to an end. The cities suck it in and spit it out. At night the winding queue sometimes comes to rest in front of the huge screens at drive-in movies or in amphitheaters where symphony orchestras are playing. But next morning the pursuit of fun, relaxation and excitement begins again; the pilgrimage to the land of leisure continues. The locust swarm moves again and leaves an altered landscape behind it. These are the Americans of the mid-century. They are a nation on a laborious search for leisure.

"A nation on wings and wheels, we have more free time than any other people in history. This is the blessing and could be the curse of a progressive and successful civilization." This was said by the 36th President of the United States. But no one ever saw Lyndon B. Johnson twiddling his thumbs. He even turned the neighborhood barbecue on his Texas ranch into a powerful political affair. In his apparent fear of letting free time go unimproved, the President mirrored fairly accurately the anxieties of a large number of his countrymen. They undeniably have much free time. But the majority of them pursue the search for fulfillment of their leisure hours with a fervor and seriousness that disclose a nagging sense of guilt. Their Puritanical inheritance apparently stirs in them. It hinders them from enjoying their free hours with naïveté; the devil finds work for idle hands—so it was once said and so it is still said by the older generation.

The Puritan ethic sees the successful mastering of work as a task "pleasing to God." But in an economy based on a high consumption of cosmetics, golf balls and nylon stockings there would be terrible crises if the "work ethic" of the New England forefathers should come into favor once again. So the inhabitant of the New World consumes with as much fervor as he once worked, and searches for the fulfillment of his free time with the same fear of failure that distinguishes him in his profession.

RARE is the American who achieves a balanced mixture of work and leisure. President Eisenhower could be cited, perhaps, as one example. Neither urgent matters of state nor international crises kept him from swinging his golf clubs when he felt like it, or doing oil paintings from photographs. The work of his staff was arranged more in accordance with his "leisure needs" than with the requisites of the Cold War. The majority of voters took no offense, but there was an undercurrent of concern about so much leisure in high office and it crept into

PETER VON ZAHN, born in 1913 in Chemnitz, Germany, was educated at the university in Freiburg, where he received his doctorate in history in 1939. Becoming a news correspondent with the German Army on the Eastern front during World War II, he went into radio broadcasting after the war and came to the U.S. in 1951 to launch a series of programs, which won wide notice, on U.S. life and politics. The author of four books about the U.S., he is now a television producer based mainly in Germany.

the political debates of the 1950s. The official defenders of the 18 Presidential holes finally had to plead that, after many hours of sitting in the Oval Room of the White House, the body needs exercise and the mind needs relaxation and recreation.

That one could use leisure time less to charge the batteries for new work than to fulfill life as such was rarely mentioned in these debates. Only recently has this viewpoint occasionally appeared in the numerous studies of the increasing amount of free time available to Americans and what they do with it. For the most part, however, Americans reject this hedonistic view and continue to believe that time outside of the job or profession should be spent primarily to renew and strengthen the forces needed for practice of the job or profession. The 40 million who ply the waters in boats, the 36 million fishermen and 39 million bowlers, the 20 million hunters and sharpshooters, and the innumerable baseball fans are too busy having fun to articulate this practical viewpoint. But relaxation from work for work—that is the unspoken assumption of the majority. And this harmonizes with the Puritan heritage.

BUT many inherited traits are crossed in the American national character. The attitudes brought by the pious men of the *Mayflower* to New England were different from those brought ashore at the James River in Virginia. Today, in Virginia's Loudon County, the horsemen in red coats who gather behind the pack of hounds are not relaxing from work but seeking through mastery over the horse and the exercise of a code of conduct that special fulfillment of life that belongs to an older, aristocratic epoch. The New York or Boston baseball fans, who seldom miss one of their idols' games and spend their coffee breaks excitedly describing the third inning, do not, on the other hand, conform to the ideas that hovered in Thomas Jefferson's mind. They are not resting for their work, or quietly using their free time to improve their minds, but are exciting themselves to the point of hysteria over the tragic ups and downs of their club.

These ball fans are in large part the descendants of the immigrants who filled the industrial suburbs of the big cities, who had broken their ties with the Old World. Now dependent upon themselves in unfamiliar and strange surroundings, they have sought groups with whose fate they can identify, with whose heroes they can exult—and over whose defeat they can fall into deep despair. The colors and emblems of their clubs have the same kind of symbolic meaning as the coats of arms and banners of Europe did for their fathers. What conflicts of loyalties arise when Casey Stengel retires, when Rocky Colavito is traded or when the entire club migrates to the Pacific Coast!

In Europe the most popular outdoor sport is soccer; in America baseball and football arouse the most enthusiasm. Why exactly baseball, and why football? Why do they mean more to millions of Americans than work in the factory or behind the drugstore counter? Perhaps it is partly because the citizens of the New World cannot escape, even in their free hours, something from the early days of capitalism that seems to have got into their flesh and blood: the urge to measure, calculate and compare.

Soccer is a game of continuous movement that at the most permits counting of goals. But the strict formality of baseball allows the performance of each player to be measured absolutely in a plethora of statistics and percentages. A good many of the male spectators on the hard seats keep detailed account of the game on score cards. Those at home are intensely interested when the television announcer observes that not since 1916 has a left-handed pitcher pitched as many shutout games in one season. When at the end of the year their favorite team has greatly improved its standing in comparison to the Senators (which does not usually take much doing), the numerous hours in the ball park can be seen not to have been spent in vain. Television quizzes have shown the extent to which fans retain the most detailed knowledge of their favorite sport. Contestants with unusual memories for baseball scores have acquired national renown.

EVALUATORS of the American character would do well to consider what pleases the citizen of the New World in his spare time. It is not the blood that flows in bullfights, nor the battle of cock against cock, that delights him, but rather the careful assessment of force against force and idea against idea. The games he loves are full of pauses, of deliberation, of strategic moves. All this makes baseball and football seem boring to the uninitiated European. There the warriors stand, armored, with visors down; they put their heads together; they bend down and remain in concentrated silence. Or they casually swing bats and playfully throw the ball around. And nothing happens—or so it appears. But then suddenly it has happened and is over before the eye can grasp it. An explosion of energy, a deep, lusty cry from the fans, and already calm quiet rules again. In sports, as in conducting war, Americans prefer an alternation of long, circumspect preparation and lightninglike action. The constant "war of motion" is not to their taste—it does not permit evaluation and analysis.

The training of players and the structure of the games mirror again the Americans' talent for organization. They lead the world in this. They have reached the stage at which, with an increasingly limited expenditure of manpower, the machine achieves high production and yields great profits. The returns are used partly for more salary and purchasing power, partly for more free time. The blessings are mixed, however. During the past 100 years the work week of the American has sunk from almost 70 to about 40 hours. But has the number of free hours really increased accordingly?

Let us disregard top management, which probably works harder now than before. But the average 40-hour worker also suffers from a series of annoying, and mostly new, demands on his time. He must travel greater distances to and from work and the streets are more often congested. He feels the pressure to continue his professional education. In order to raise or maintain living standards, many more women must work than was the case a century ago. The "own home" that has been obtained by a good half of all American families needs constant care. The lawn must be mowed, flowers tended. There are almost no personal servants—only the mechanical slaves in the kitchen and basement that like so much to break down. All of these demands diminish the theoretical number of free hours in the week.

STILL, what Lyndon Johnson said is correct: "We have more free time than any other people in history." In any case the Americans have more time "off the job"—and even if one subtracts the hours spent in sleeping, eating, shaving, washing hair, driving to the supermarket and taking the children to ballet school, there are still so many hours left over that an American family can spend an average of more than four hours daily in front of the television set. They can spend it in shifts if they wish and with interruptions for telephone conversations with the chairman of the PTA—but still there are some four hours of free time each day, four hours that can be filled sensibly and profitably or foolishly and worthlessly. Four hours in which one can spend one's money in an absurd or graceful manner, or save it, or increase or lose it in a game of poker.

AMERICANS not only have more time but also more money than any other people to use for their leisure. The National Recreation Association published figures indicating that in 1960 $40 billion —approximately 10 per cent of the national income —was spent for "fun." Twelve and one half billion of this was spent on trips within and outside the United States, and as much again on the tools of the increasing "do-it-yourself" industry. It is difficult to determine exactly how large the figure for "fun dollars" really is. Does it include the expenses for new, powerful cars that are a prerequisite for the American world of leisure? Or the billions that are spent on cigarettes, soft drinks and liquor? These also are not unessential elements in banishing boredom.

A Puritan from the 17th Century would turn over in his grave if he heard of such spending. But at least he would be happy to learn that the importance of spectator sports has diminished relatively in comparison to free-time activities that demand more than mere watching and filling out score cards. Passive onlooking has been transferred to the television screen in the living room. The desire, the money and the free time for a more individually spent leisure have grown: America is becoming a nation of sailors, tennis players, hikers, bird watchers, swimmers and divers, hunters and fishermen. The possession of one or more cars per family has made everyone mobile. For the worker whose father knew only the way to the ball park, the auto has made accessible suburban golf courses, the parks in the Rocky Mountains and the sandy shores of Florida. Thanks to the two-day weekend and the paid vacation, the American landscape has become a paradise where millions of city dwellers can delight in their own physical existence.

The urbanization of America (three out of every four citizens live in a city environment) has started a movement that is fulfilling Jean Jacques Rousseau's "back to nature" concept—and on an unprecedented scale. Every year millions of Americans throw off their city clothes and dress in plaid shirts and blue jeans, ready to camp alongside a trout stream in the Alleghenies or in a state park near the Great Lakes. Few of them return to the style of Daniel Boone and the pioneers of American legend. Their air mattresses are pumped up with the fumes from the exhaust of the station wagon. An electric razor and a small refrigerator are hooked up to the car's cigarette lighter. The tent has a window and an electric light. Their ancestors would hardly have acted otherwise had they possessed this equipment. After all, they, too, were practical people. If they could have spared themselves the daily hunt for elk and bear by opening a can of food, they would have done so.

BUT what surely would have amazed the early settlers is the modern camper's need to stay as close to other campers as possible, to pitch his tent on a parking lot with public telephones. The modern American is not the restless individualist who broke camp when he saw the smoke of a strange campfire on the horizon. He belongs to a generation that tends to judge a campsite according to whether one can find an evening game of bridge or a square dance in front of a communal fire.

And it is no longer just the men who fill their free time with physical exertion and imagine they are seeking the simple life in the manner of Thoreau. Women have taken over the camps. They transform them into polished outposts of civilization that include electric hair driers and insect-repellent sprays. And they, especially they, seek company, contacts, the opportunity to meet "nice" people. In the American view, people are nice until they have proved themselves otherwise. It is difficult enough to recognize American class differences in any sort of leisure activity; in camping, differences in origin and income are blurred beyond recognition. A truck driver and his family can camp next to a junior executive from United States Steel. By the time the Primus stove has exploded for the second time the women are calling each other by their first names. It is fairly certain that the trailer belonging to the oil worker from Texas will be more luxurious than the one rented by the State Department official from Washington.

Any American can join the army of leisure seekers. Well, almost any American. The only one who has difficulties, whether he be a university professor or a wealthy doctor, is the one whom a loving God brought into the world with a dark skin. The races in America are even more segregated during leisure hours than during work. It is not without reason that the Negroes fought and are still fighting with such bitterness for equal rights to use swimming pools, tennis courts and motels. And since men tend to reveal more completely their innermost selves during leisure hours than during their work, the antipathy between the races is more clearly visible in the organization of free time than during the 40 hours in the office. Moreover, one of the main activities during free time is establishing relationships with members of the opposite sex. The taboo on intimate contact between white and Negro makes integration during leisure time that much more difficult.

The less well-off inhabitants of Harlem or of Chicago's South Side therefore spend their leisure in ways largely different from the white man in the green suburb. The pattern of ghetto leisure harks back in some respects to the 19th Century. For example, the church plays a larger role in determining leisure-time activities. Church services offer a release for pent-up emotions, and other church activities provide a sociability and warmth that are otherwise not easy to find in the harsh life of big Northern cities.

In association with the church, and imitating the deeply ingrained organizing inclination of white Americans, all sorts of societies flourish. There are Negro clubs corresponding to the Elks and Rotary and Shriners that combine sociability with good works. But below the respectable bourgeois level of this club life, a high percentage of dark ghetto inhabitants have leisure hours inflicted on them by the lack of jobs. Some spend this demoralizing leisure in aimless ways: in dice playing and the numbers racket, in as much smoking and drinking as a limited supply of money allows.

THERE are some signs, however, of hopeful change, especially in sports. The great Willie Mays trained his batting eye on the makeshift baseball diamond in his Alabama hometown, but now Negroes are coming forward in sports that need special, costly equipment. Charles Sifford is a regular on the professional golf "tour." Althea Gibson and Arthur Ashe have become superb tennis players.

If, except in certain athletic endeavors, skin color separates the nation during its leisure hours, television tends to unite it. The "TV" unites teenager and senior citizen, man and wife, laborer and merchant, the rich and the unemployed, East and West, and, what is more difficult, North and South. That American television can occupy so much of the free time of a great and diversified nation does not have as much to do with the number of programs as with their uniformity. They are uniform above all in their lack of controversial content.

Thus they do not offend—and they please the great masses because they are for the most part very well done. Uniformity is demanded by the advertisers who finance this enormous system, and they serve up to Americans the paradox of a changeable monotony. Four or five channels hammer side by side at the viewers 17 hours a day.

T HE innocence of the programs is, of course, relative. Observers from other continents would, after one week of studying juvenile delinquency and the obtrusion of sex and crime on the American scene, blame television. In doing this they forget that the constant violence in Westerns belongs to the national legend. Crime and the detective have a long history in Anglo-Saxon literature. Television has had as little effect in spurring the law-abiding citizen to illegal action as Punch and Judy shows had in determining Hitler's mania. One confuses cause and effect when one holds television responsible for the American fascination with sex. Sex, crime and violence have always had their place in American life.

Defenders of American television even see advantages in the frequency of violence in programs. In this way, they say, the viewer has an opportunity to relieve his aggressive instincts through vicarious experience. One asks oneself, though, if the American national character is really so aggressive that it needs to be cleansed through four hours of entertainment a day. In reality, sensitivity is dulled by the innumerable acts of violence in dramas and cartoons. The American people spend an incalculable number of leisure hours in utterly passive contemplation of extreme situations.

During the Kennedy Administration the chairman of the Federal Communications Commission spoke about the "vast wasteland" of television, implying that American television in its present form is not providing an experience of lasting value. In large measure he was right. However, television is not by any means totally barren. The efforts of the

large networks to bring dependable, on-the-spot political reports to the public are most praiseworthy; at times American television has served the nation truly like the assembly of Athenian democracy. Before and during the Presidential elections, at times of great race conflicts or in foreign-policy crises it has been an excellent medium of information. In the documentary films of Fred W. Friendly and Edward R. Murrow it reached a level of political journalism that could hardly be surpassed. It has aided in unmasking demagogues like the late Senator Joseph R. McCarthy. The 90 noncommercial educational channels make it possible for Americans to learn what science teaches and the arts offer. If one compares the number of regular viewers of such programs with the number of those who watch the common entertainment shows, however, one is not surprised by the average American's underdeveloped knowledge of political reality. Never has a series of educational or informative programs been included among the top 10. One must conclude that most Americans turn on their television sets almost solely for entertainment, without reflection and without aftereffects, good or bad.

T HE critics of American television demand perhaps more than it can achieve—and also more than is offered by European television organizations, which do not have to exist from the sale of time or depend for program choice on general public taste. However, the persistent uneasiness about television in America's articulate and intellectual circles must have some meaning. Furthermore, even the average television watcher does not seem to have a completely clear conscience. If he did, he would want to have even more viewing time, and this, apparently, he does not want. On the contrary, according to a poll conducted by George Gallup, the greater number of Americans are of the opinion that the relationship between working and free hours should not be changed substantially in favor of the latter.

Even among the industrial working classes one meets with opposition to the idea of reducing the 40-hour week to, say, 35 hours. The prevailing opinion seems to be that men would not really know what to do with more free time. Many wives do not want their husbands sitting around the house any more than they already do—they consider it more of a curse than a blessing. And they suspect, probably rightly, that with more time off the men would stop devoting time to the dirty dishes or the poison ivy behind the rosebushes and would squander their paychecks at the race track.

Puritan tradition is of course suspicious not only of leisure but also of adventurers and fortune hunters, cardplayers and gamblers. But America has a frontier tradition as well. Frontier life was erratic, sometimes bringing hard work and danger, sometimes days of idleness, sometimes poverty and sometimes pockets full of silver dollars. Luck and chance played the biggest roles on the Western frontier. The man who constantly had to defend his existence against weather and wilderness, dangerous animals and unfriendly Indians, calmly played for high stakes during his leisure hours. He who wonders about the leniency with which America tolerates its gambling dens must take into account this old frontier tradition, which constantly wars with the Puritan tradition. It is not just the rich and idle few who seek through gambling to inject excitement into their too-long leisure time. Anyone who takes a walk along the Strip in Las Vegas meets a sociological cross section of the New World—not the best perhaps, but nevertheless a cross section. The American does not yield to his fate—he seeks it out and challenges it.

Except for those working on the lowest rungs of America's economic ladder, Americans are subject to strong competition in their working lives. An improvement in social status as the goal of existence has been part of the American Way of Life for a long time. The man who does not "make it" blames not the unfriendly forces in his environment but only himself. Even the hours of leisure are not completely carefree. They, too, are spent with an eye on the social status one hopes to reach.

HOUSEWIVES play this game with no less energy than men, and sometimes with more. Their headquarters in the campaign for social recognition is their house. This is not the European stronghold in which the family spends its leisure in seclusion. It is a label and advertisement. The average housewife cannot stand to see the Joneses install a new and better kitchen with an electronic grill. A garbage-disposal unit must be purchased to prove that the race is still on. When the appliance breaks down—well, the husband has set up a workshop in the basement that hums and buzzes with the machinery of the do-it-yourself age.

What a happy mixture of well-being, social competition and joy in creating new things! And the less useful the ash trays and vases, the bookshelves and lamps that are produced in these countless busy basements, the more fun there seems to be in making them. Aristotle, who thought a great deal about leisure, would see his ideal fulfilled, after a fashion, in many suburbs of Chicago or Philadelphia: an involvement of the mind and spirit with beauty without the expectation of any practical application.

THE involvement, of course, is tremendous. Today's job in office or factory seldom brings anything new in which the worker can fully participate, and in a world which dissects work into small, apparently disconnected pieces, the creative drive remains unsatisfied. More and more Americans fill this void with glass painting, pottery making or abstract sculpture—or with reweling the fittings of a dinghy. Grandma Moses gave hundreds of thousands the courage to try oil painting. A nation of Sunday painters and sculptors has arisen.

So has a nation of music makers. We do not mean the music that constantly trickles into rooms from hidden holes or that teenagers find on the radio as an accompaniment to their mathematics homework, but music that makes demands: classes, finger exercises—at least attentiveness and the ability to discriminate. Phonograph-record sales indicate how many admirers European classical music has won in the New World. There are 1,300 symphony orchestras in the United States, and they are seldom supported by states or cities; usually private donations make possible their existence. It is no longer just popular music that accompanies free time—it has serious competitors in Bach and Bartok. Beneath this musical plane, Americans have rediscovered in their leisure hours the broad, half-forgotten field of folk music, from hillbilly to the Irish ballad, from the Negro spiritual to the pious revival songs of West Virginia. This music tells more clearly than songs of other peoples the story of the development of a diverse nation. It is not only the growing interest of the Americans in their own past that has caused this wave of folk music—it is also their need to sing along, to make music themselves in a time of mechanical music. And it is more than that. The guitar has become a type of political instrument. Youth gathers at hootenannies and demands in song equal rights for all—black and white.

Although the white people of America have on the whole shown a lamentable lack of hospitality to their black fellow citizens, Americans nonetheless are a convivial lot who love to "have people in." The great distances of early times that automatically made any stranger a guest have diminished, but the wide-open door has remained. Even in this good custom, however, there is some of the competition that penetrates all phases of life in the New World. At a party the person who can introduce a man from faraway places—if possible someone with color slides of Burma—has triumphed over his neighbor.

THE inclination toward sociability with complete strangers has found its apotheosis in the phenomenon of the cocktail party. As is well known, it is important at these parties to exchange the fewest possible thoughts with the greatest number of people in the shortest amount of time. Of all free-time activities the cocktail party is the most exhausting for the housewife because she must constantly stir the sluggish soup of conversation and give every guest the opportunity to meet the guest of honor. It is also exhausting for the guest because he has to shout to make himself heard by the person opposite him (whose name he did not catch). The host has it the best: he only has to fill the glasses. By 9:00 p.m., when the last guest has departed an hour too late, what exhaustion, but, at the same time, what bliss to have entertained the executive vice president! The great expense of money and effort is proof that the leisure time was used properly.

Fear of not using leisure properly is almost as strong as the fear of failure in one's profession. This double fear drives many Americans, as we said before, to fill their leisure time with activities that aid their advancement in society and profession. Nowhere do so many people voluntarily participate in evening classes or correspondence courses. And nowhere do people so often undertake good works for social or business reasons. Men head fund drives and their wives do volunteer nursing in hospitals in many cases because these can increase status and reputation in the community.

Underlying such activities is, however, above all a real desire to do something for the neighborhood and the congregation. According to the American interpretation, leisure time belongs not to the individual alone but also to the larger community in which he lives. It is easy to find volunteers in America, not because they have so much time but because they look on their leisure hours as not wholly their own. When it is a question of forming a committee to change the zoning regulations, to save an old oak tree from the bulldozer or to collect children's clothing for Congolese refugees, the American women are there with ardor and a talent for organization. One look at the women's section of the local newspaper shows how many volunteer activities bedeck the American woman's free time.

Sometimes it seems as if the American's greatest hobby is not collecting stamps or breeding poodles but politics. Public affairs occupy the American's mind even when he permits himself leisure. He does not theorize about the best form of government, for he believes his country already has it. As a pragmatist, politics is for him a case of personal cooperation. The Presidential election campaigns engage the free time of hundreds of thousands of Americans for eight months. What other nation would enjoy spending so much of its leisure time going through the motions of naming a leader whose selection is often already assured? Leisure in a dictatorship is time that the state believes it can grant to its subjects. Leisure in a democracy is opportunity to divert energy for the benefit of society.

THE pursuit of happiness is a task given the American by his ancestors at birth. Leisure spent in quiet contemplation does not belong to his happiness. Leisure must be organized, must bear fruit, must be successful. The *vita contemplativa* does not grow well in American soil. Leisure is a function of life for Americans, not its goal. Alexis de Tocqueville was already aware of this 130 years ago when he said of the American: "If his private affairs leave him any leisure, he instantly plunges into the vortex of politics; and if at the end of a year of unremitting labor he finds he has a few days' vacation, his eager curiosity whirls him over the vast extent of the United States, and he will travel fifteen hundred miles in a few days to shake off his happiness. Death at length overtakes him, but it is before he is weary of his bootless chase of that complete felicity which forever escapes him."

In the gray early morning a fisherman, who plainly prefers to avoid vacationing herds, surf casts on Washington's Olympic Peninsula.

The People's All-out Attack on Their Free Time

Americans devote almost as much energy and ingenuity to filling their leisure hours as they do to their work. With the fervor of a crusading army they beat off the threat of an idle hour. Reading, thinking, doing nothing—these often seem to go against the national grain. Tens of thousands of New Yorkers take jets to Miami Beach even if they only play cards when they get there. Millions torment themselves with the perversities of putters on golf courses or with balky tents and stoves on camping trips. A restless civilization that resists rest, America will never decline through apathy: it may just drop from exhaustion.

AT A CARD TABLE on a terrace of the Fontainebleau Hotel in Miami Beach, older guests play gin rummy while, in the background, several women learn yoga.

BESIDE THE POOL of a Miami Beach hotel, vacationers from the North soak up the sun *(left)*. In a typical year Miami's tourists spend more than $350 million.

ASTRIDE A ZEBRA strategically placed in front of a motel, visitors have their trip recorded for posterity *(below)*. There are 382 hotels and motels in Miami Beach.

ALONE IN THE SUN, a guest savors a moment of solitude on "Tahitian Beach," a strip of waterfront owned by the big $12-million, 17-story Doral Beach Hotel.

EXPENSIVE FUN of various kinds is offered on luxurious charter boats, beside mammoth swimming pools and at elaborate night clubs

PALATIAL POOL of Chicago's Riviera Club *(below)*, part of the exclusive Outer Drive East Apartments, has a 3,600-square-foot sun deck with adjoining cocktail lounge. Businessmen who rent the more elaborate cabanas pay up to $1,650 a year.

BIG FISHING BOATS wait at a dock in Miami Beach for well-heeled fishermen to rent them at a cost of $75 a day. The boats are equipped with all the gear necessary for catching sailfish and marlin, which abound in the waters of the Florida coast.

GARISH SUPPER CLUB on the roof of Miami Beach's Doral Beach Hotel *(below)* holds 500 customers who have come to eat costly meals and dance to Guy Lombardo's orchestra. Other bands, such as Count Basie's, play in another dining room.

RODEO SITE, the town of Spray, Ore. *(above),* has a population of about 200 people, most of whom make their living raising cattle. The town's popular annual rodeo grosses about $10,000.

FEARLESS GIRLS spur on their mounts *(left)* in the rodeo's Open Women's Race. Professional rodeo riders are banned from the Spray Rodeo, which attracts about 100 participants.

LEAPING COWBOY bulldogs a steer *(below)* in one of the rodeo's more dangerous events. After jumping from his horse he must wrestle the horned, wildly thrashing steer to the ground.

OUTDOOR CHEFS at Fishing Bridge Campground in Yellowstone Park build campfires between trailers and cars. Some 220,000 trailers and other camping vehicles were sold in 1964.

BOY SCOUTS at Fishing Bridge use tents *(below)* instead of trailers, but still fail to achieve wilderness solitude. Some U.S. campgrounds are surrounded by laundries and restaurants.

GREGARIOUS YACHTSMEN, members of the Seattle Yacht Club get together at Port Madison on Puget Sound for their annual "potlatch"—an Indian word meaning "a gathering of people." Among the events that take place while the boats are tied up is a dinghy race *(foreground)* among contestants who handicap themselves by putting their heads in paper bags.

DEDICATED OUTDOORSMEN, *undaunted by drizzles and the cold light of dawn, doggedly pursue the pleasures of the vigorous life*

DETERMINED GOLFER grimly faces a wood shot from a rain-soaked bare spot on a New York area public course. The area's public courses are so crowded that golfers rise at 4 a.m. to play.

INTENT BIRD WATCHERS, members of the Massachusetts Audubon Society *(right)* trudge through a Cape Cod rain in hopes of spotting some of the Cape's many unusual species.

Dr. Norman Vincent Peale preaches to a packed congregation at Marble Collegiate Church in New York. Dr. Peale is known for

132

...bular books asserting that a positive attitude is the key to success.

An Optimistic People's Religious Zeal

by MAX WARREN

THE religious scene in the United States of America is one of almost bewildering perplexity to a foreign visitor. Never is it more true than in religion that a traveler, after saluting the Statue of Liberty, must leave his past behind as he explores this land of the future. For a European thinks countrywise—if he is English it will be islandwise—but the United States is continental in its scale. And this is true not only in terms of square miles but in the enormous variety of its population.

It is vitally important to keep this continental perspective when attempting to analyze the specifically religious life of the nation. And the same perspective is also necessary in order to appreciate the dimensions of what is in its nature a tremendous spiritual undertaking, the creation of a national unity out of many disparate elements. For within the borders of the United States there is taking place the most exciting experiment in racial mixing anywhere in the world. No one who in the least degree appreciates the perils in which mankind stands today—not least the peril of a civil war in which humanity may come to be divided on racial and color lines—will doubt the spiritual quality of the

"American Dream." By this I mean the dream of a society in which every individual is to be treated as worthy of respect not by virtue of ancestry or ability or wealth but simply as himself or herself; a society in which all are equal under a law that is the expression of a common will, not something imposed by arbitrary authority; a society in which a man's religious convictions or lack of them are respected as being his own concern and responsibility upon which no legal limitation can be placed; a society worthy of transforming a continent and proving an inspiration to all mankind.

But paradox haunts the alien observer from the start. For while it is true that the visitor from Europe must forget his past, his own background, and refuse to allow it to be the standard by which he judges things in this country, yet history, the past, is a clue to the United States as to every other country. Four factors in that past are important for understanding the religious scene.

The United States is the greatest of those nations for which an immigrant past is a living fact in the present. There is a sense in which the myth of the Pilgrim Fathers obscures the reading of history instead of illuminating it. The Pilgrims who landed in New England were not the first immigrants. It is easy to forget that another migration had already begun to take place from Africa, bringing with it not only problems for the future but also a spiritual contribution not less distinctive than that of the Pilgrims. Later, in Europe, the devastation of the Napoleonic Wars unsettled large masses of European peasantry who sought peace and prosperity across the Atlantic. The desperate tragedy of the Irish potato famine brought another huge influx, which was in turn followed by large-scale emigration from Italy.

Religious America has been composed of many diverse traditions: the Puritan and Reformed tradition with the religious significance it gives to secular affairs; the Baptist and Quaker tradition of vigorous independency; the Lutheran tradition that holds fast to the 16th Century doctrinal Reformation; the Roman Catholic tradition of liturgical worship and a highly centralized organization; the Anglican tradition of liturgical worship and decentralized organization; the Methodist tradition of flexibility for evangelism; and, subtlest of all, the tradition of African folk religion—each of these came to add its distinctive ingredients to the American melting pot. Cynics have claimed that the only thing that melted was the pot! But, as this chapter will aim to show, that is not really even a fraction of a half-truth.

THE second factor that has served decisively to shape the religious scene in the United States has been the frontier. In a real sense the principle of "disestablishment" in religion, which has been so integral a part of the national attitude toward religion, derives in no small part from the moving frontier—that frontier which for the best part of the 19th Century was never still, being pushed ever westward. And it was those religious bodies that most vigorously followed the frontier as it moved, in particular the Methodists and the Baptists, which set the pattern of American religion.

The Congregationalists of New England and the Episcopalians of Virginia and the Carolinas had in a real measure established themselves in something like the old European pattern. They were so well established, so anchored by their roots, that they failed to move. And so the Methodists and the Baptists, with their evangelistic zeal and flexible organizations, their impatience of convention and their "go-getting" determination, captured the frontier. Their individualism, the flexibility of their ministry and the adaptability of their Church order suited the conditions of frontier life in the period when the United States, forgetting its colonial past, moved toward its "manifest destiny" as a great power. As a result the "typical" citizen of the United States, the man or woman who poses for the foreign cartoonist, the type we aliens think of as characteristically

MAX WARREN, Canon of Westminster (England), was born in Dublin in 1904 and studied at Cambridge University. In 1927 he went to northern Nigeria for a brief tour as a missionary for the Anglican Church's Church Missionary Society. After a time as Vicar of Cambridge's Holy Trinity Church, he became the General Secretary of the Church Missionary Society, serving in that capacity until 1963 and making many trips to the U.S. Among his books are *The Christian Imperative* and *Challenge and Response*.

American, is likely to have Methodist or Baptist forebears if he not one of them himself.

A third factor that contributes to the contemporary picture of religion in the U.S.A. derives from the recent past: it is the immense mobility of the population. The frontier may have reached the Pacific; immigration from abroad may have been greatly reduced; but within the nation, movement is continuing. "A new car every year, a new wife every two years, and a new house every three years" is another cynicism that can be largely discounted, but it does point to a phenomenon whose religious significance must engage our attention. Twenty years ago Willard L. Sperry, Dean of the Divinity School at Harvard University, wrote in his book *Religion in America:* "We are a mobile and migrant people, dwellers in flats and apartments. 'Moving Day' is a recognized national festival"; then he added, "but the day of long moves is over."

How wrong he was! Far from the "long moves" being over, the shifts of population from East to West, from North to South and from South to North have changed the whole population picture of the country dramatically, with political repercussions that cannot yet be assessed and with religious results that are far-reaching.

A FOURTH factor, and one not readily appreciated by the usual visitor, is the peculiar constitutional pattern of the nation. The United States is a union of states. However great are the perils of the contemporary scene, the responsibilities of the nation as a great international power, and some internal problems that make for the strengthening of the central Government in Washington, the main tensions within the nation stem from the relations of the individual states to the Union. One of the bloodiest civil wars of modern times was a struggle about this question. It bedevils every program that deals with issues of social justice, whether these concern the registration of Negro voters or medical care for the aged. And, what is important for our subject, this insistence on the rights of each unit in the Union affects the religious scene also. Methodists in Texas or New Hampshire, highly disciplined as a denomination though they are, cannot be directed rigidly from Louisville, Kentucky. Episcopalians in South Carolina and California will be found to act with marked independence of many advices

that come from New York. National denominational conventions find it extremely difficult to reach decisions. And few myths are more vulnerable than that of the monolithic structure of the Roman Catholic Church. Los Angeles, St. Louis and Boston speak with very different voices.

This would seem to be the religious reflection of the political organization of the nation.

I have stressed these four factors on the ground that religion is part of life, and it is impracticable to try to isolate spiritual elements from their sociological and political environment. It is the interplay of all three that make the man.

K EEPING all these considerations in mind, a few generalizations can be attempted as clues to the understanding of religion in the U.S. today.

The most obvious fact that strikes the traveler is that, apart from those religions that are indigenous to the United States, or first took shape there—such as the Mormons and the Christian Scientists—every major religious grouping has links with some comparable denomination in Europe. But as soon as the traveler penetrates beyond the first surface impressions, and after he has survived the warmhearted welcome that he will invariably receive, and has been allowed to look around, he will discover that the denominations have suffered a real sea change in crossing the Atlantic. Forms of worship may be recognizably similar, but there is a subtle change of atmosphere, hard to pinpoint but unmistakable.

By this change of atmosphere I mean something much more than the warmth and friendliness that are almost overwhelming to those acclimatized to the frigid aloofness of so much church life in Europe. This is a change that can be attributed to the racial amalgam of the American people and their emancipation from the hierarchically organized societies of the Old World. The change of "feel," however, is due to developments in American life that markedly distinguish the pattern of religion in the United States from that in Europe.

In Europe the structure of religious life is still dominated by the fact that socially, if not legally, one particular church in almost every country enjoys a measure of privilege not accorded to the others. The complete absence of this element of ecclesiastical privilege in the American scene is a factor of enormous importance in assessing the character of religion in the U.S.A. One immediate result of this is the ease with which men and women of different religious traditions work together in community projects. This in turn helps to explain the steady increase in ecumenical cooperation at the local level, and as a result the great part played by Americans in the Ecumenical Movement throughout the world.

One interesting sequel to this lack of any privileged position for one denomination is that distinctive American phenomenon, the Community Church —a church that is not even labeled denominationally. Its minister may be a Methodist at the moment, a member of the Disciples of Christ a few years later, and then a Congregationalist or a Baptist. This again explains the ease with which, in the United States, men and women move from church to church. Nothing comparable to this is to be found in Europe.

THIS might appear to suggest something superficial in the character of American religion. But that would be a grave misunderstanding. Religion determines the way an American thinks and acts every whit as profoundly as it does the man or woman of any other part of the human race. What is different is the fluidity in American religious life, which stems from the fact that the idea of any one religion having some right to pre-eminence is totally absent from the religious consciousness of the American. Beyond doubt there are plenty of citizens of the United States who are convinced that their particular religious beliefs are right as against all others. If you doubt that, you have only to discuss such matters with a Southern Baptist, a Missouri Synod Lutheran or an Irish Roman Catholic in Boston. But in so far as these have become assimilated within the American tradition they will not ask for themselves nor grant to others any position of privilege in the common life. The absence of any religious "Establishment" is a matter of principle, part of the American Dream previously mentioned.

Yet, interestingly enough, this absence of an Establishment of religion is combined with a remarkable public veneration of religion. Writing more than 75 years ago in his book *The American Commonwealth,* James Bryce could say what is as true today, that "all religious bodies are absolutely equal before the law, and unrecognized by the law, except as voluntary associations of private citizens. . . . So far from suffering from the want of State support,

religion seems in the United States to stand all the firmer because, standing alone, she is seen to stand by her own strength."

There are many illustrations of this. The fact that the state exempts all church property from taxation, in so far as it is used for worship and religious education, may not be unique but at least it might fairly be interpreted as a tacit vote of confidence in the role of the churches in the nation's life. The fact that the two houses of Congress have chaplains and that their sessions are formally opened with prayer is another indication of the dignified place given to the public and official recognition of religion.

One notable result of the lack of any form of religious Establishment is the general absence in American life of any substantial anticlericalism—at least among Protestants. Indeed, it can be argued that the honored place accorded the minister in the life of most communities is the positive complement to this negative fact.

Perhaps at this point one may be permitted to hazard the belief that the dramatic revolution that has recently taken place in the mood of the American Negro, and his confident struggle to assert his place in the nation's democratic life, is a religious phenomenon, one that still calls for analysis. There are those who would say that the religion of the American Negro is a folk religion only thinly veneered with Christianity. The notable leadership of Negro ministers of religion in their people's struggle, and the distinctively Christian character of this leadership, would suggest that this is a superficial judgment. All that I would stress at this point is that the leadership in practical action has been to a very significant degree that of ministers. A popular revolt led by clergy is a rare phenomenon in modern history. Perhaps it could only happen in the United States, where it is quite unthinkable that the clergy should be in any sense a privileged caste.

A SECOND generalization about American religion is that it is characterized by individualism. Let me explain what I mean in this context by the word "individualism." I do not mean individualistic. In religion, as a matter of fact, Americans tend to be very conformist. Nor is this due to the many forces in American life today that generate conformity, such as the influence of mass media, the prevailing pattern of "Organization Man," the subtle pressures

A CAMP MEETING, depicted in a lithograph from the 1830s, shows the religious fervor that swept the frontier in the early 19th Century. The revivalist tradition has remained part of the U.S. scene, with such preachers as Billy Sunday and Billy Graham, and the spirit of evangelism, of which the camp meeting was an extreme manifestation, remains strong in U.S. Christianity.

implied in the idea of "Fortress America" or even the much more noble aim of the "Great Society." All of these contribute to conformism in American life. But the conformist tradition in American religion is due to the fact that essentially it is "small-town" religion, neighborhood religion. The good neighbor in America is happiest when he is like his neighbor.

The individualism of American religion is the individualism of the local group. The American is first and foremost a member of his local congregation, and only then of his denomination. This is at once a source of strength and a potential source of weakness. Because its accent is laid on the neighborhood, on the individual congregation, it is a binding influence on the life of the local community. In part this harks back to the frontier days when it mattered supremely that a man knew who his neighbors were and could trust them. The religion that captured the frontier was a religion peculiarly suited to the local situation. Distances were great in those days and communications difficult. A religious group had to depend on its own resources. This made for independence, for the growth of many denominations. And each independent congregation had a strong and vital life of its own.

But another influence has come in to strengthen this emphasis on the local church. The great movement of internal migration that we have seen to be a contemporary phenomenon has resulted in multitudes of people moving into new areas. The need to know one's neighbor lies very deep in the mores of

Americans. And there is the need of the children to know other children. In these new communities, these communities of so many newcomers, the church is the most obvious place where a recent arrival can get to know people quickly. This goes some way toward explaining the phenomenal fact of a steady growth in church membership in the United States. For at least 150 years the records show that the percentage of the population actually affiliated with the various Christian denominations has gone slowly but steadily up and today represents 60 per cent of the population of the country.

A sense of proportion demands that we remember the other 40 per cent. This includes the significant Jewish minority. And to them must be added the adherents of the ethnic religions of Asia. All of these are part of the religious picture of America—professing and practicing men and women of religion. We must not, however, forget that many among this 40 per cent either profess no religious belief at all or cannot with a good conscience identify themselves with any religious denomination.

Despite the social role of the Christian churches in the U.S., their large memberships cannot be dismissed as a sociological fact without spiritual significance. It is easy for the cynic to say that the churches are simply a religious variation on the Elks and Lions of the business world or on the fraternities and sororities of the universities. It is equally easy to contrast the evidence of church attendance (which is commonly very high indeed), and of the astonishing generosity with which Americans support their churches, with the evidence of a breakdown of traditional moral standards that can be cited from the Kinsey Report and the statistics of divorce and remarriage. The cynic can indeed point to all sorts of discrepancies between theory and practice, between church attendance and actual social ethics. But then he always has been able to do so. Yet this must be said, and it is very important to insist upon it, that the social and political life of America is built upon a strong neighborhood sense. And a decisive element in this—one of the most powerful forces of cohesion in American life—is religion. The American, if he is religious at all, feels that his church belongs to him. Incidentally it is something for which he is prepared to pay. What is more he likes to know what he is paying for. One direct result is that the American layman has a very great say indeed in running his church's affairs and in determining the way in which his church influences the community life.

HERE is one incalculable source of strength in American religion. Leaderless it could run out into the sand, but the religious scene in America does not at all suggest a lack of leadership at this important local level. The individualism of American religion, as here defined, tends to produce leadership. An uninhibited laity not only keeps the ministry awake but inspires it.

Having said all that to the credit of this congregational or local-church emphasis, one must also say that it has its weaknesses. Small-town religion can be very parochial; it can be very insular in its understanding of what religion is meant to be as a force in the national life. Small-town religion, overpreoccupation with the local scene, can very easily lead to religion becoming nothing more significant than a local cult. Or if it ventures out more widely it can become little more than enthusiasm for the American Way of Life. There is, of course, nothing peculiarly American in this danger. But it is a danger that needs to be reckoned with.

As a third generalization there is the indomitable optimism that characterizes American religion. This optimism takes innumerable forms and is a characteristic alike of the churches of the Atlantic seaboard, the fundamentalist groups of the Middle West and the sometimes fantastic sects to be found in California—and indeed of everyone, even of those

evangelists who, from the deepest conviction, adhere to a presentation of the Gospel which takes a radically pessimistic view of human nature.

This optimism, so dramatically in contrast with the prevailing religious pessimism of Europe, is essentially a psychological and not a theological fact. At the very heart of the American Dream, no matter how it has been formulated, has been the conviction that America is "the land of opportunity." And no traveler who has moved extensively over the country; who has flown from Chicago west to the Rockies and looked down on the patterned landscape of Iowa and Nebraska, where not so long ago was wilderness; who has seen the cultivation of the Salinas valley in California; who has driven across Tennessee—to mention three glimpses that could be multiplied a thousandfold to illustrate what can be done with nature when man has the courage and the will—no such traveler will doubt that in an astonishing way the dream has come true. From this springs the religious drive of the man who says that if you want anything badly enough you can get it. It is no accident that in the church advertisements of any American newspaper you will readily find such a statement as "Revival will begin at the First Baptist Church next Sunday at 6 p.m." In more sophisticated circles it will be expressed very differently, but the inner conviction will be the same.

THE immense material development of America and its outward and visible prosperity (if one does not look too closely) have hitherto gone far to afford an apparent justification for this optimism. Church statistics of membership and material resources point in the same direction. In consequence there is a naïve belief that organization, "know-how" and money are all that are really needed to remedy almost any situation. That may seem a cruel generalization, but as a generalization let it stand. I have heard it put more crudely and forcefully by many an American. Ironically, many Americans are prepared to accept the generalization as true but are no less determined to prove it false; and precisely for this reason it is possible to view this boundless optimism as being something that is authentically rooted in the Christian tradition and can by that tradition be redeemed from its superficialities and illusions. This general optimism coexists with, and is not contradicted by, much genuine self-criticism and an increasing recognition that the churches must rethink their place in American life.

From these generalizations, dangerous as all generalizations must be, let us turn to look at the immediate scene. The United States is the foremost world power of our time, and no assessment of the religion of the people of the United States would be adequate that failed to take into consideration what that religion has to say about the position of the United States today.

The history, tradition, culture and religion that America shares with Western Europe are, indeed, unifying factors. But there are "straws in the wind" today which suggest that the Atlantic Ocean may become a barrier rather than a bridge. Western Europe seems to be turning in upon itself, becoming in a curious way isolationist. Its retreat from its onetime cultural, economic and political dominance of the world and its deep-seated loss of spiritual conviction together constitute a divorce from the past. There is little sign that Western Europe, of which Britain of course is a part, knows where it is going or even where it wants to go. This in turn has had its influence on the United States, which seems to have acquired a mood of disillusionment. The rest of mankind does not appear to be very responsive to American leadership and certainly shows little appreciation for America's phenomenal generosity from the Marshall Plan down to the annual appropriation of vast sums for the aid of the underdeveloped countries. In the new accent being placed on achieving within the United States itself a further development in the realization of the American Dream, there could be a new kind of isolationism.

THESE are but "straws in the wind." Events may cause the wind to veer. Certainly there is no cause as yet for alarm on either side of the Atlantic. But the fact that serious students of affairs are thinking like this argues the need for religious insights to be brought to bear on the situation.

In this respect it is possible to insist that what men and women have made of their religious faith is a factor of very great importance indeed. In America the religious faith of many has led them to take a world view of their nation's responsibilities, a world view that completely transcends what at this moment or that may be held to be the particular self-interest of the nation. At its finest and deepest

the religious consciousness of the American, and not only of the Christian American, makes him a world citizen. It is here that reference should be made to the great foreign missionary activity of the churches of the United States. When it is remembered that for multitudes of Europeans emigration to America was an escape from intolerable conditions in Europe, it is hardly surprising that the average American citizen, before the age of tourism, saw the Atlantic Ocean as a providential bit of geographical insulation shutting him safely away from involvement with the rest of the world.

THE significant exception to this way of thinking was that minority of opinion in all the denominations that was dedicated to the foreign missionary enterprise, an enterprise that began before there was an American Way of Life that anyone thought worth exporting.

In the first half of the 19th Century, apart from a limited number of persons engaged in commercial enterprise, the United States was represented abroad almost exclusively by missionaries. This explains that long association of missions with the foreign diplomatic service of the U.S.A. which is unique in the annals of the worldwide missionary movement. Many missionaries, even while still serving in their religious capacities, were in the 19th Century vice consuls if not consuls of their country. Their daughters married into the consular service. In this way a tradition grew up that much influenced official American thinking. It was no accident that the last United States Ambassador to China who was able to represent his country in Nanking had begun his service in China as a missionary.

There is not much exaggeration in the claim that it was the influence of the missionaries that created whatever international outlook there was in the United States until the end of the 19th Century. What is important is to realize that the same influence has helped cushion the shock of disillusionment caused by the debacle of United States policy in China. Someday it may well be recorded that this magnificent resilience of the missionary-minded, after the devastating events in China, contributed in no small degree to preserving a public opinion strong enough to support successive Administrations in giving material aid to underdeveloped countries. Certain it is that missionary influence has played a significant part in encouraging the great philanthropic organizations of the United States to contribute very significantly to countless projects for the welfare of the peoples of Asia and Africa. Nor can it be easily estimated how enormous has been the direct American missionary contribution to the entire missionary enterprise throughout the world and, indeed, to the Ecumenical Movement as regards both personnel and money.

CYNICS, and there are plenty about, will dismiss much American philanthropy as being nothing but judicious schemes designed to prevent the spread of Communism. What, however, cannot be seriously disputed by any who know the facts is that the great outpouring of human energy and self-sacrifice by those concerned with the foreign missionary task has derived primarily and fundamentally from the Christian conscience. This outward-going movement of the spirit is one of the great creative contributions of American religion to modern history. It is a contribution in which all the denominations have shared, as well as countless individual missionaries who have been sent to Asia and Africa and Latin America as the "love gift" of some individual congregation—often a quite insignificant one in terms of the number of its members—which was determined that its own small-town religion would have a global perspective. When the chips are down it will be the American Christian who will prevent his country from retreating into "Fortress America" or being satisfied with a "Great Society" limited to the North American continent.

Less spectacular than the missionary outreach but scarcely less important in its potential is the immense amount of experiment being undertaken by religious groups within America itself—experiment toward meeting the needs of the new "frontiers" inside the United States. The integration of the Negro with his fellow citizens is one such frontier, as difficult and sometimes as dangerous as the Oregon Trail and the Badlands of the Dakotas in earlier days. The problem of the "inner city" in the vast conurbations of the United States presents another frontier. There are also the programs for helping juveniles and young adults to adjust to society—the problem of "youth" as it is called—programs that are being promoted in all parts of the United States. Meanwhile, the immensely vital intellectual life of

the nation, its thrust toward outer space and down into the depths of man's own individual and social roots, is calling out a response in the field of American theology that may yet put the creative theologians, the Christian thinkers of America, into the leadership of Christian thinking throughout the world.

What may perhaps be discerned within all this religious vitality is a search for some new way by which ordinary men and women can become more responsible citizens of their own country and of the world. The nursery period of American history down to 1776 saw a pattern of religious life dependent on the European model even when in reaction against it. The beautiful little Connecticut townships of Litchfield, Washington and Woodbury, for instance, while obviously *of* America, are yet unmistakably redolent of England. "Adolescent" America, with its bursting energy that conquered the West, produced the campfire revival meetings and created the Main Street mentality of small-town religion. We have seen just how wide-visioned and heroic Main Street could be. Today a great nation is finding itself in a new role as the arbiter of fashion in culture and in so much else for *all* mankind. We sometimes forget that the Soviet Union and China and everyone else, whether they admit it or not, are fascinated by the United States and are trying to catch up. The international arbiter of fashion in ways of thought and living must find a new religious expression, for it would be the ultimate tragedy for the United States to gain the whole world and lose its own soul.

NO one can foretell what this new religious expression will be, except that it will be something very different from the expressions that were given to religion in the past. Of this we can be sure, because the American genius is the genius of the pioneer. The quest is on. The vitality in American religion today may yet make it a prophet not only to America but to the world. The idealism that is so pregnant a feature of American religion may yet purify the materialism into which America and all mankind is sinking. The pioneer spirit of American religion holds out the promise of fulfilling in new fashion the Biblical vision of a highway being prepared in the wilderness of human life. This may not be America's manifest destiny, but it could be its actual one.

Father Carl Donovan leads a religious procession into the neighborhood streets of his largely Puerto Rican parish in Lorain, Ohio.

Church Groups Vigorously Fighting Social Evils

Americans manifest an unceasing drive to better the lot of their fellow men, and it is through their churches that they most often organize to relieve such problems as poverty, racial discrimination, slum conditions and juvenile delinquency. A good illustration of American churches in action is found in Lorain, Ohio, a Lake Erie industrial city of 75,000 shown here and on the following pages. With many Puerto Ricans and Negroes, as well as impoverished whites, Lorain in the mid-1960s was confronted with most of America's urban problems. Recently its churches have been mobilizing to find solutions.

RACIAL BARRIERS *are attacked by ministers' groups trying to persuade industry to end discriminatory job practices*

STEELWORKERS head home from the big Lorain plant of U.S. Steel *(above)*. The 20-member Mayor's Human Relations Committee, led by Congregationalist minister John Huston, has helped the plant find competent Negro office workers.

WHITE WORSHIPERS kneel in Lorain's Pentecostal Church of God *(left)*, a storefront church attended mainly by poorer whites. Most of Lorain's churches remain, in practice, segregated, primarily because they serve specific ethnic groups.

INTERRACIAL GROUP, the Lorain County Conference on Religion and Race meets at a church in Oberlin, Ohio. Established in 1963 to promote racial harmony, the conference has grown to include 400 clergymen and lay leaders.

JOB COUNSELING is given Mrs. Jean Wofford by Rev. John Huston *(left)*. Although a trained legal secretary, Mrs. Wofford had been unable to obtain a job in Lorain. Church-run employment assistance is breaking down such race barriers.

143

VISITING LAYMEN, members of the Roman Catholic St. Vincent de Paul Society, a charitable organization, call on a poor Puerto Rican family in a Lorain slum district to give out money for food and rent.

ACTIVE CLUBWOMAN, Mrs. David Manwell gives out clothing to a poor Negro family. Her group, the Lorain Woman's Club, operates a Clothing Bank with the aid of the First Congregational Church.

SOCIAL-WORK PROJECTS *backed by the churches bring help to the needy of Lorain*

AN INSTRUCTING NUN tells two mothers about baby diets at the outpatient clinic of Catholic St. Joseph Hospital, which serves the whole community. The clinic gives free medical care to welfare patients.

ELDERLY WOMEN chat in the lobby of Lorain's Firelands Retirement Center. The center, backed by 17 Lorain County Protestant churches, provides low-rent apartments for men and women over 60.

AN ANCIENT CEREMONY *brings the church directly to a Puerto Rican area*

A WORTHY FAMILY receives a procession that has come from the Chapel of the Sacred Heart, Lorain's largely Puerto Rican Catholic parish, during a Corpus Christi celebration.

Following an ancient Spanish custom, the procession visits the homes of the two or three most deserving families. Then the priest has an altar set up on the porches and blesses the people.

ENTERTAINING AN INMATE, four ladies of the Lorain County United Church Women give a birthday party for a girl in the Lorain County detention home. Mrs. Peter Smith *(far left)* began this service.

LEADING A PICNIC, Tom Peters takes another of his boys' clubs, "The Counts," to a nearby lake *(below)*. Peters came to Lorain to work for Catholic Charities, was later hired by United Community Services.

RUNNING A CLUB for boys called "The Spades," young social worker Tom Peters holds an informal meeting behind a barn *(left)*. Peters directs Lorain's United Community Services Special Youth Project.

READING IN CLASS, three children concentrate on their studies of the Bible and of other subjects at a vacation school run by the First Lutheran Church of Lorain. These summertime classes are integrated.

Graduation ceremonies are held on the football field at St. Olaf College as seniors and their guests hear a commencement address by Art

Education's Growing Dilemma

by HERBERT VON BORCH

8

...rson, a former special assistant to President Eisenhower. St. Olaf is a small, coeducational liberal arts college in Northfield, Minn.

THE word "education" has always had a magical sound for Americans. It is at the root of the American value structure, because American society, unlike the European, is based on the idea of universal feasibility. Deeply rooted in the American consciousness is the notion that anything is possible, that any goal can be reached. Men are not doomed through gross and ineradicable imperfections in their nature—what theologians call original sin—to live lives that are tragically unfulfilled if not downright sordid. The American view is not so rosily optimistic, of course, as to hold that man is perfect. But there is a distinct belief that he and his society contain a virtually inexhaustible potential for self-correction.

A more illuminating expression of this fundamental American conviction could hardly be found than a statement made by John Dewey in his *Reconstruction in Philosophy:* "Not perfection as a final goal, but the ever-enduring process of perfecting, maturing, refining, is the aim in living." And education is the religiously revered instrument of this perfectibility. This attitude was part of the philosophical foundation of the nation. The French and English rationalists of the 17th and 18th Centuries had insisted that man was not condemned by God to a life that was "nasty, brutish and short." Rather, they believed that through learning and the diffusion of knowledge man could improve himself and control his environment. The statesmen who wrote the Declaration of Independence, such as Thomas Jefferson, Benjamin Franklin and John Adams, were students of 17th and 18th Century rationalist thought.

Not only did the nation's founders believe that man was rational and educable, but they could not have formulated the American Constitution, posited as it is on the benign and rational cooperation between men, had they not held this hopeful belief in the essential goodness of man's nature and in the efficacy of education. They *assumed* that if the new nation was to survive, an educated electorate was necessary. Jefferson spoke for them all when he said: "If a nation expects to be ignorant and free . . . it expects what never was and never will be."

This faith in, even reliance upon, education has not died with the years; if anything it has become stronger. It has had a profound reaffirmation during the Administration of President Lyndon B. Johnson in the Government's decision to assign to education the long-term job of resolving the problem of "structural" poverty. Education has thus become an indispensable instrument of social and economic change, a weapon in the "war on poverty," the chosen method of solving the toughest national problems. Lyndon B. Johnson's ambition is to be remembered as the "Education President."

Further, the United States sees the answers to the problems of the "technological revolution" in terms of education. Workers displaced by machines are to be retrained on a massive scale to operate these machines or to find other work. The looming "problem" of leisure has come under the Government's purview. Better instruction in the humane subjects so that Americans may more intelligently use their free time is among the nation's declared aims. In short, the United States, long committed to the ideal of universal education through the high-school years, now looks forward to a vast expansion and improvement of its entire educational effort. President Johnson has said that the country's aim is "excellence" and that everybody who can profit from college-level instruction ought to have a chance at it. An astonishing ambition—and yet it is entirely within the realm of possibility.

THESE wide as well as lofty aims, reflecting a view of education as the means to social and human perfectibility, have no exact parallel anywhere in the world. The educational systems of the nations of Europe characteristically aim at a high degree of "excellence," but only for a small proportion of the population. Although Britain and France are trying to widen educational opportunity, only a small proportion of European youths attending state schools —some 15 to 20 per cent—go on to "grammar schools" or other institutions that will give them the preparation they need to study at a university. The rest—supposedly the less gifted—complete their formal education at about the age of 14 and are expected to get jobs and go to work. The elite that receives preuniversity training is further winnowed by such famous and terrifying examinations as the French school system's *baccalauréat*.

The students who successfully run this gantlet, qualifying for and then completing preuniversity studies, have received an excellent education, better than that offered by all but the top American secondary schools. And many of these successful students are from poor families. But many are also from families wealthy enough to have given them extra educational advantages. The European system thus has tended to perpetuate an aristocracy of wealth and learning.

In contrast, the American political philosophy of freedom and equality has engendered the goal of the

HERBERT VON BORCH, author of a widely respected book on the U.S. entitled *The Unfinished Society*, was born in Swatow, China, in 1909, the son of the German Minister to Peking. After studying at the Universities of Berlin and Frankfurt and receiving his doctorate from Heidelberg in 1933, he became a newspaperman. In 1950 he founded the monthly *Aussenpolitik*. Since 1966 he has been U.S. correspondent for the German newspaper *Süddeutsche Zeitung* and has traveled extensively throughout this country.

public high school accessible to all—a uniquely American phenomenon—with correspondingly higher participation in university-level studies. Two thirds of all American youths graduate from high school and more than one third go on to college. As the Rockefeller report of 1958 puts it, the American political ideal has "heaped upon our educators one of the most heroic assignments a society could have invented."

The truly staggering proportions of this "heroic assignment" have become increasingly evident in the last decades as U.S. educators have become more and more aware that simple universal education is not enough. What is to be done with the gifted child, for example? Is he to be left in the same classes with average and below-average children where at best he will waste time and at worst become bored and resentful? Or is he to be put in special classes with other fast learners, thus becoming a member of an educational elite? Clearly in this complex age the U.S. has decided that it cannot afford to waste any of its brain power through failure to inspire and inform its most intelligent young citizens. On the other hand, is it compatible with the American ideal of equality to single out for special treatment those who happen to be gifted? The dilemma can be reduced to the following terms: on the one hand, can a free society be truly egalitarian; on the other, can an egalitarian society also be free for the development of the above average, that is, of the gifted?

THE first question, really, is whether the tremendous natural and social distinctions existing between students in any given community can be bridged at all. Students from poor and undereducated families find it difficult to compete in school with the children of educated parents. The curious result is that public schools, which seek, democratically, to give the same training to all, are unable to educate the underprivileged up to a level where they can compete for jobs and thus escape the poverty of their parents. In short, the free development of talent —equality of opportunity—simply perpetuates inequality. Poverty resulting from undereducation is handed down from generation to generation; it is self-perpetuating. This paradoxical problem has been recognized, and its solution is one of the aims of the antipoverty drive. It will take a long time to

reconcile this strange conflict between freedom and equality; nevertheless, new education legislation has made a beginning.

The second question, whether an egalitarian society is compatible with freedom for the gifted, has been dramatized since the launching of the first Russian Sputnik in 1957. That triumph in outer space heightened the doubts about the effectiveness of U.S. schools that had already been plaguing American educators. The question really goes to the heart of the great experiment of American education and must be seen in historical perspective.

THE history of U.S. education, in fact, mirrors the history of the nation as a whole. American educational institutions have responded to the various stages in the country's development—the emancipation from colonial domination, the actualization of the principles of the Declaration of Independence, the exigencies of the frontier, urbanization and industrialization, the influx of immigrants, the overwhelming influence of a society shaped by economics and finally the wave of self-examination that has marked American society in the 1960s.

In the colonial period America's nascent system of schools and colleges was loosely modeled on that of Britain. English class distinctions were maintained: elementary schools were for the lower classes, secondary schools (the "Latin grammar school") for the upper. The first college, Harvard, was founded in 1636 primarily to provide Puritan Massachusetts Bay Colony with a supply of clergymen, but it was conscious of a direct link with Cambridge University in England and shared with the other early colleges, such as William and Mary (1693), the ambition to produce "educated gentlemen" in the aristocratic, humanistic tradition. In line with traditional English practice the first American colleges were founded not by any governing authority but by voluntary associations, almost exclusively of a religious character. But their idea was not egalitarian.

Although few children had any extended formal schooling in the colonial period, the idea of the public elementary school had emerged by the middle of the 17th Century. These public schools did not wipe out private and church-run schools, which continued to flourish, as they do to this day. The transition to an authentically American educational system set in after the War of Independence. The system inherited from the Old World, based on distinctions of class and religion, was regarded by the new nation as no longer adequate to the beliefs that had brought the United States of America into being. For Thomas Jefferson, education was essential to democratic self-government; he could not foresee the contradiction between the principle of universal education on the one hand and the "natural aristocracy" of talent, in which he also believed, on the other. The difficulty of harmonizing the humanist tradition of an intellectual aristocracy with American society—a conflict barely perceptible in colonial days—was implicit in that contradiction; it was the real germ of the "crisis" in American education that arouses so much discussion today, 200 years later.

Political equality led logically to the establishment by the middle of the 19th Century of the public, nonsectarian elementary school, supported by general taxation, as the American norm. The process of democratization soon extended to the creation of free public high schools that offered courses preparatory to college. By the time the Civil War began there were already more than 300 of them. This was the first step on the road to the comprehensive high school of the present day.

THE expansion of the new nation led also to the creation of another group of distinctive American educational institutions, the "land-grant" colleges. Departing from the English tradition of voluntarily endowed universities, the federal Government in 1862 passed the Morrill Act, which authorized states to set aside grants of Government land for the establishment of agricultural and technical colleges. These state colleges proliferated prodigiously and are in large part responsible for the fact that the United States today has almost 1,500 institutions of higher learning, including approximately 145 universities, 790 liberal arts colleges with four-year courses, 60 technological colleges and 185 teachers' colleges. To a European these numbers are staggering. Great Britain, although it has a number of technical colleges, possesses a total of only 31 universities and has no institutions comparable to the U.S. liberal arts colleges.

Also disconcerting to a European is the disparity in the quality of university education in different parts of the country and even in different institutions within one state. Part of the explanation lies in the varying amounts of money that the different states can allocate to education. Another reason is the absence of any qualitative norm, any agreed-upon standards. Still another is simply that quality attracts quality. If it becomes known that a state university has a good French department, bright young instructors of French will want to teach there. The French department will become excellent, and this will pique the English department to strive for greater quality—and so on. A number of state universities offer instruction of the highest order. The elite Berkeley campus of the vast, state-wide University of California, for example, rivals and perhaps in some fields surpasses such renowned old institutions as Harvard and Yale.

AMERICA'S endless diversity or, as a cultural sociologist has called it, its "capacity of ambivalence" has also become distinctive of the high school. "When one tells a foreign visitor that we have tens of thousands of local school boards with vast powers over the elementary schools and the high schools," writes James B. Conant in *The American High School Today*, "he is apt to say, 'This is not a system but a chaos.' To which I always reply, 'But it works; most of us like it.'"

A further stage in America's growth had a profound effect on the country's educational system, on both its aims and methods. As the frontier was pushed westward, political equality began also to mean equality of opportunity, and this promise drew streams of immigrants into the country. This, in turn, placed upon the American schools responsibilities wholly unknown in Europe: millions of children of barely assimilated parents had to be brought up to be American citizens, and the public and parochial schools became an agency for eliminating the distinctions between minorities. This they could hardly do by sticking to a classical curriculum confined to literature and the sciences. So it came about that the American school child was expected to learn social relations, good manners, the rules of the democratic game and civic-mindedness along with a smattering of Shakespeare and algebra. The needs of society came first, and the child was not so much educated as socially "adjusted."

This trend received a decisive impetus at the beginning of this century from the teachings of John Dewey, the philosopher and Columbia University professor. Dewey's "new pedagogy" revolutionized American educational practice because he sought to move it away from the classical authoritarian approach and adjust it to the needs of students living in a complex modern world. He advocated, to take a simple example, that rather than lecturing—telling students what to think—teachers should hold discussions to which the students could contribute their own ideas concerning the world around them. Education, according to Dewey, should not give the student just a theoretical, textbook understanding of the world, but rather do everything possible to immerse him in his environment. Dewey's "progressive" education, when applied with intelligence, let a good deal of air and sunlight into stuffy classrooms, but it reduced the importance of the humanist curriculum that had been an integral part of the American school system. Certainly nowhere has the psychological and sociological approach to education, as compared with the academic approach, been carried so far as in America.

Unfortunately, many of Dewey's followers placed far too literal a construction on his dictum that education should be a part of life. In their opposition to the old "Alexandrian" approach they neglected academic subjects in favor of "social adjustment." School curricula became anarchical: courses in cooking and interior decorating were given the same importance as courses in mathematics or medieval history. Physics and marriage counseling were placed on the same footing.

A REACTION against this anarchy began to set in as early as the 1930s. A neoscholastic movement, whose most influential exponent was Robert M. Hutchins, emphasized the necessity of "basic education" and denounced anti-intellectualism and the idolizing of the "practical." This movement slowly gained momentum and by the 1950s parents at PTA meetings were insisting on a return to harder, "old-fashioned" teaching methods. Americans were thus prepared for the merciless soul-searching about education, and especially about the adequacy of U.S. science instruction, that has been going on since Russia orbited its first Sputnik and proved itself a formidable rival to the U.S. in scientific learning and achievement.

The country's immediate reaction to Sputnik was to call for more engineers and scientists. In this call many Americans were implicitly demanding that education serve not truth but the needs of the state. Fortunately, after the first furor died down, a wide and constructive debate began. From this debate have come a number of reforms that amount to what is often called "a revolution in the classroom."

Among these reforms is a whole new attitude toward the nagging problem, discussed briefly earlier in the chapter, of what to do with gifted children. For many decades American sentiment was so firm that the educational system's first task was to serve society—to imbue young citizens with all the proper patriotic sentiments—that little thought was given to the possibility of encouraging genuine intellectual adventuring. Indeed, the educational system, overwhelmed with an ever-increasing number of immigrants and other young people from every social level, did not have the facilities to engage in special programs. Further, any such schemes would have seemed to many at least vaguely subversive of the American egalitarian ideal. In order to bring off the tremendous experiment of providing secondary education for all without prior selection on the basis of performance, the whole of American educational theory centered around the average or even the less-than-average child.

BUT to recognize a crisis is the first step toward curing it. The United States Office of Education has given official sanction to the new policy of encouraging gifted students: "Today it is important to face the challenge of preventing talent loss within the current school process, particularly of the gifted and the creative. After forty years of attempting to reach all secondary school youth, we now have recognized that the creative and the gifted persons are the most likely to be overlooked in the comprehensive secondary school. The challenge for us, then, is to find the proper place for these pupils." The egalitarian goal has not been discarded, but Jefferson's belief in the natural aristocracy of talent has now come into its own as well.

America, moreover, has found its own method of selection on the basis of talent, a method altogether different from that prevailing in either Communist or non-Communist Europe. The American method is designed to avoid creating any veiled class distinctions; it is to be generous, clement to the majority, never rigid or mechanical. What America is attempting in its high schools—in many of them, at least—may be described as a talent selection conducted as painlessly as possible: painlessly for the majority of average students, but painlessly also for the gifted, since they are preserved from becoming a distinct, arrogant caste.

Thus, even after the traumatic shock of Sputnik, America has preserved its identity. And after a good deal of educational soul-searching, the country has likewise declined to subordinate the humanities to the sciences. More engineers are indeed being trained, and space projects are swallowing up still more funds. But the goal remains a "humanist" culture. To a European it is disconcerting that humanism should have more champions in the U.S. than on the continent of its birth. Some years ago A. Whitney Griswold, the late president of Yale, remarked sadly after a trip to Europe: "A brief educational pilgrimage to Britain, Western Germany and France soon convinced me that we could no longer count on those countries to keep alive the pure flame of liberal learning they lighted eight centuries ago."

EAGER RECRUITING of college graduates by U.S. industry is spoofed in a cartoon by James Flora. In comparison, high-school graduates—and dropouts—are much less sought after.

The soul-searching that led to a revolution in the high schools has produced markedly better-prepared freshman classes in the colleges. Higher intellectual standards have prompted colleges to liberalize their curricula. These reforms may be described —with all due caution—as a "re-Europeanizing" of the American university. It is characteristic of this approach to regard study as an "active" rather than a "passive" process. Instead of marching platoons of students through four uninterrupted years of

lecture courses, each course tied up neatly with a "final exam" at its end, colleges have begun to experiment with independent study programs in which students can omit some course work and do research projects of their own. Such programs are presently in operation in 520 colleges and 122 junior colleges. Albert Einstein once remarked that it was nothing short of a miracle that modern methods of scientific instruction had not strangled the "holy curiosity of inquiry." To revive such curiosity American universities are returning to a concept that goes back to the great medieval universities, the concept that a mature student should prepare, "on his own, through reading, travel, attendance at lectures as he chooses, and by conversations with tutors, fellow students and perhaps even barmaids and idlers, for a set of examinations he will be permitted to undertake when he considers himself ready." This, indeed, is the way most university students still study in Europe, and if the system appears to lack the crisp efficiency of courses and quizzes, it encourages the good student to do valuable creative work.

THE momentum of the higher birth rate, combined with the unprecedented expansion of many fields of knowledge, has called forth other experiments in education. To cope with both types of growth, important changes in curricula and teaching methods have been introduced in the last decade and a half. Textbooks on physics, chemistry, mathematics, biology and English have been drastically revised with the aim—which John Dewey would have approved—of encouraging students to seek answers of their own rather than memorizing formulas. A textbook reviser has said on this score: "Instead of just learning how to use the old mental tools of technology, built by someone else, students in the new courses are taught to build the tools they will need to deal with circumstances which will arise. That's the only way they will be able to cope with the new knowledge that is coming along so rapidly."

The technological revolution that has produced the rapid expansion of knowledge has also produced new methods of facilitating the learning process of the constantly growing school population. What is known as programmed instruction, by means of "talking typewriters" or "teaching machines," helps students to learn to read and spell more rapidly. Television has become an established medium of instruction. Some 650 closed-circuit systems are operated by educational institutions, and millions of students in schools and colleges are taught in part through this medium. Other hopeful experiments include "team-teaching," which reduces the problem of overly large classes; the elimination of rigid divisions by age groups so that pupils are permitted to move ahead as rapidly as they are able to; and a de-emphasis on grades, which many teachers feel hinder teaching and create a bad spirit, leading even to such abuses as cheating and plagiarizing.

THE classroom revolution that began in the 1950s is one more proof of America's potential, as a young, unfinished society, for "self-correction." Nevertheless, it has thrown into relief a revealing paradox in the American attitude toward education. More than ever before Americans are setting great store by education. Its social and economic values have always been highly rated, and now it is seen as the magical elixir that will ultimately enable the nation to stand off the threat of Communism. How, then, is it possible that a scholar such as James B. Conant should charge his people with not taking education seriously? The answer is that however highly Americans may have prized education, they have not, in the past, attached sufficient importance to it as an end in itself, as a value unrelated to usefulness. This, in turn, may result from the fact that Americans are not inclined to recognize absolute cultural values that transcend the goal of individual self-fulfillment in a well-organized society. To do things for their own sake—art for art's sake—is not characteristic of the American approach to life.

Paul Tillich, the philosopher of religion, touched the essence of the problem when he said that should the universities lose their function of seeking truth without compromise, should they be transformed into research laboratories for industrial purposes, then industrial development itself would come to a standstill, for ultimately industry depends for its new techniques and inventions not on applied science but on the disinterested search for truth. The Russians' scientific breakthrough in space brought Tillich's dictum home to America's educators, and the shock that Sputnik inflicted upon the American consciousness has already borne good fruit. Nevertheless the danger remains that America, as Mr. Conant says, is still not seriously enough

committed to learning for its own sake. The crisis in American education is not caused by the possibility that America has produced fewer engineers than the Soviet Union. Nor does it come from within the ranks of teachers who, humanists and scientists alike, are allied in their determination to foster the "holy curiosity" of free and pure inquiry. The crisis instead is the product of the very structure and temper of American society.

We can call it industrial society or, with Walter Lippmann, the "Jacobin" democracy, or even the free society. Whatever its name, it is the social element, the most significant formative force in American life, that has subjugated education. For every nation has its distinctive genius, and even if America in the 20th Century has performed gigantic industrial and technological feats, its distinctive genius has shown itself in the society that has developed on this great continent in the course of three and a half centuries, its freedom secured by the checks and balances of power, with its staggering material productivity, its increasing classlessness, its exciting mobility. This society, in the consciousness of Americans, appears to have assumed a virtually divine character. This, far more than technology, is the power that brooks no absolute values beside it, even the absolute value of truth. The crisis in education is therefore synonymous with the question of what an all-powerful society has done to the arts and sciences.

THE pressure of society and its demands can easily be perceived in American classrooms. At an early age the school child learns to think in sociological categories: family structure, the group, the municipality, the democratic process. He learns about unions, the business world, population problems, politics. But does this sociologically oriented education—originally given impetus, as we said earlier, by the need to assimilate the children of immigrants—achieve its purpose of producing thinking adherents of a social order based on freedom? Therein lies an as yet unresolved dichotomy. An education directed toward civic loyalty, toward a certain form of American nationalism, is little suited to promote the critical approach essential to the free play of forces in a democracy. As Christopher Jencks wrote in *The New Republic:* "The ideology of the public schools (and to a lesser extent the public colleges) is majoritarian; minorities are to be 'assimilated' if they are ethnic, to be ignored if they are religious, to be distrusted if they are socio-economic."

Other pressures exerted by society are militating against the liberal arts. The humanities and theoretical sciences are being increasingly elbowed out of college life by vocational courses in subjects like business management, which have an obvious and immediate relevance to life in modern America. In 1964 almost five million students attended colleges and universities, and the figure is expected to be 10 million in 1980. The egalitarian principle that as many as possible should attend institutions of higher learning has become an explosive force. The requirements of society therefore have ripped open the colleges and universities both spatially and as regards curricula. The liberal arts tradition has not been undermined by the growing importance of technology, as might have been supposed. What has happened is that economic and commercial forces have effected something in the nature of a silent seizure of power within the academic world. The technical colleges, particularly business, agricultural and engineering colleges, have siphoned off ever-increasing numbers of even the most gifted students.

In fact, a close alliance between the university and business has become a distinctive feature of American academic life. Only a small minority of students still take degrees in traditional subjects, and the sciences are just as affected by this trend as the humanities. Some 20 per cent of all graduates major in business and commerce. These students are channeled directly into the big firms, which send their recruiting agents onto the campuses in order to secure the services of the future graduates even before they have completed their studies.

BUT a change appears to be setting in. An anti-business climate has developed in universities like Harvard, and business recruiters are finding it harder to fill their quotas. "I want work that is meaningful," said a recent Harvard graduate, and another summed up the attitude of many of his classmates by saying, "I am not sure that business is for me." Businesses themselves are changing their attitudes. Some of the more farsighted large corporations are pressing the universities not to strangle the liberal arts and sciences by excessive and early departmentalization in business subjects. In short, even the giant corporations, supposedly the citadels

of American materialism, now have come to see that what is good for the country is good for them, namely the development of tolerant, well-rounded people with training in the humanities.

It appears, in fact, that present trends in education represent in many ways a return to certain fundamental positions. We can view the history of the American experiment of universal education as a great circular movement. The settlers who came to the New World brought with them humanist traditions of education. The purpose of this education was to produce the cultivated gentleman. When these settlers founded their own republic after the War of Independence, in order to establish a free and egalitarian society, they set out to offer this humanist education to everyone. But as education was subordinated to the needs of the egalitarian society, these ideals came into inevitable conflict with the factor of numbers. The masses streamed into the high schools and colleges.

MEANWHILE, this egalitarian society had become consumer-conscious, pleasure-seeking and unimaginably productive. Its momentum had transformed education to suit its own tastes. And one day the discovery was made that the ideal of the cultivated gentleman had been quietly set aside in favor of that of the conformist young manager, socially well adjusted, psychologically trained for leadership. Courses in the techniques of industrial management, sales, publicity and scientifically elaborated customer manipulation had taken priority over other subjects. Greek had turned Carthaginian.

But now a return swing of the pendulum in the "Greek" direction seems to be taking place. America has realized that, even from the most empirical of all viewpoints, that of power and status in the world, it must not scorn intellectual curiosity, the independent reflection of the solitary, perhaps even asocial, introvert, lest one day it find its creative sources polluted.

America, it seems, is beginning to take education really seriously, an attitude going far beyond respect for education as the panacea for social evils. Education serves society best when it is not too subservient to society, when society is not deified and when values are recognized that transcend the social.

In a sense America is thus reverting to the outlook of the Founding Fathers, the most highly intellectual statesmen in modern history.

A genial teacher, visiting Professor Philip Morrison laughs at a student response in a class at Massachusetts Institute of Technology.

Exciting Diversity of Educational Opportunities

America's devotion to learning is reflected in its great range of educational institutions. Large numbers of parochial and private schools supplement vast public school systems geared to educate the entire population. Even within the public schools there is great variety in curricula. Bold experiments in teaching are paralleled by the advanced architecture of many new schools. On the level of higher education—where institutions range from tiny colleges to renowned universities—the diversity is even greater. More and more students, many benefiting from scholarships, go to college each year. New colleges spring up and old ones enlarge as the nation seeks to extend its already broad educational programs.

AN ADULT EDUCATION CLASS given by Northeastern University includes a busy housewife *(above)* who has brought along her child. Some women drive as far as 70 miles to attend classes. Boston has many programs for adults.

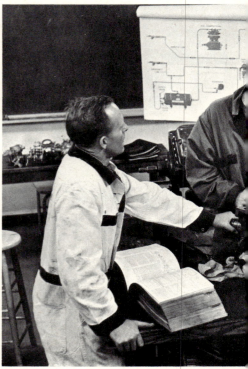

A GREAT LIBRARY, Harvard's Widener *(left)* offers excellent study facilities in its Main Reading Room. Harvard's library system contains more than 7.5 million volumes and pamphlets, making it the nation's largest university library.

A HUB OF EDUCATION, *the Boston area pours enormous energy into its variety of schools, colleges and universities*

AN ADVANCED SEMINAR on African art at Boston University *(right)* draws graduate students and faculty members to hear Dr. Alphonso Castagno. Other major institutions in the area include Tufts, Brandeis, Radcliffe and Wellesley.

A VOCATIONAL SCHOOL, Boston's Franklin Technical Institute holds classes in automotive engineering *(above)* and other industrial skills for post-high-school students. More than 1,400 students participate in part- or full-time programs.

ROMAN CATHOLIC STUDENTS at the Sacred Heart elementary school in Roslindale, a part of Boston, practice for a concert. The school, run by the Sisters of St. Joseph, has a prize-winning orchestra and maintains the high academic standards set by the education-minded Boston archdiocese.

EXPERIMENTAL SCHOOL operat by Newton's public school system e courages young students to teach a entertain each other *(right)*. Nam for the educator Horace Mann, t school is not divided by grades, b has several large teaching rooms whe a child can progress at his own ra

A FINE PRIVATE SCHOOL, Milton Academy, one of the Boston area's oldest, has a section for girls *(left)* and one for boys. Unlike most New England college preparatory schools, Milton has many day students as well as boarders. Each year more than 95 per cent of its graduates go to college.

NEW CAMPUS of the University of California, the San Diego unit joins a state-wide complex that includes 95,000 students

PLANNED FOR GROWTH, a new physics classroom *(left)* at the University of California at San Diego (UCSD) holds but a fraction of the students it is equipped to handle. UCSD is one of nine campuses that make up the nation's largest system of higher education. Only UCSD's Revelle College had been completed by 1968, but San Diego will eventually have 12 colleges.

BREEZY PASSAGEWAYS stacked up on concrete pods *(right)* connect Revelle College's Physics-Chemistry Building with a biology classroom building. Originally a school for graduate training in the physical sciences, UCSD has evolved a liberal arts curriculum, including a program for undergraduates. Its 1965 enrollment of 1,350 students will swell to 27,500 by 1995.

A HIGH-LEVEL SEMINAR is led by Dr. Keith A. Brueckner, head of the Institute for Radiation Physics and Aerodynamics at UCSD. Since UCSD's aim is to broaden traditional educational programs, it offers seminars in such varied subjects as cosmochemistry and 17th Century philosophy.

TOWERING MONOLITH, a terraced building on the Revelle College campus of UCSD is one of four recently completed multipurpose structures that contain classrooms, laboratories and offices for the science and engineering departments and the new humanities program.

STUDENTS AND TOTS take advantage of the playground and park outside the married students' quarters *(above)*. Constructed of stained wood, the handsome building offers furnished, one-bedroom apartments for as little as $115 a month.

OUTDOOR STUDY is a common sight on the patio *(left)* adjacent to the Science and Engineering Library. The campus has many such esthetically pleasing touches: paintings by students and local artists line corridors and are displayed in classrooms.

A PATIO CAFETERIA provides a sunny meeting place beside the Physics-Chemistry Building *(right)*. The open, airy quality of UCSD's architecture reflects both the contours of the land and the university's idealism, confidence and academic daring.

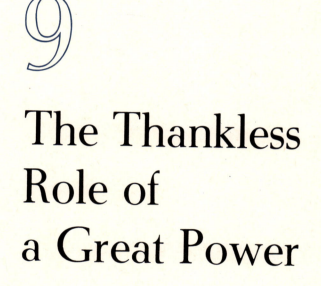

9

The Thankless Role of a Great Power

by Raymond Aron

SINCE the beginning of this century the United States has been to all intents and purposes the most powerful country in the world; yet until 1941 it neither translated its economic strength into military force nor played a role on the world scene commensurate with its potential. During World War I, for example, it did not have enough weapons for all its soldiers, and until the last few months of hostilities they used French and British arms. Even in 1940, at the time of the fall of France, the American Army looked foolish—a far cry from the one that landed in France on June 6, 1944. President Franklin Roosevelt himself did not believe that American troops could remain in Europe more than two years after victory. Yet 20 years later they were still there, and leaders in Washington were solemnly asserting at every opportunity that they would stay there as long as circumstances required. American public opinion, which in 1945 clamored for the return of the boys, today accepts the fact that they mount guard in West Berlin and on the 38th Parallel in Korea; for years it accepted their fighting and dying in the jungles of Vietnam.

Thus there would appear to have been a complete reversal in the attitude of the United States, its people and its Government, with regard to foreign affairs. This country, whose Congress refused to ratify the Versailles Treaty or join the League of Nations and whose spokesmen mistrusted commitments and entangling alliances as contrary to the interests and purposes of the country, was in a few years to become the center of a network of pacts and alliances

169

woven throughout the whole world. After having been accused of isolationism it became suspected of pactomania.

To the eye of the historian this conversion is less radical, less miraculous than it seems at first glance—or than it has seemed to the Americans themselves. Although the American Government has never subscribed to a militaristic or warmongering philosophy, the United States has been no more peaceable a nation than other states. In the 19th Century it expanded its own territory, taking possession of a virtually unoccupied continent without having to fight major wars, but without forgoing the use of force when necessary (as in the war against Mexico). After the war with Spain and the occupation of the Philippines, the United States became a power in Asia and the Pacific and could not avoid playing a major role in the conflicts in that area. Considering the world situation and its own purposes and national interests, it should have provided the means for supporting its policies long before 1940. In short, it is the country's withdrawal between 1920 and 1940 that today seems irrational and paradoxical, and not the action taken since 1945.

In other words, the United States could scarcely have escaped its fate. Because of its size and the volume of its industrial and human resources, it had become the foremost of the great powers even before 1940. From the moment that it resigned itself (or resolved) to tolerate neither the empire of the Third Reich nor the Japanese Greater East Asia Co-Prosperity Sphere, the United States was condemning itself to the point of no return from world politics. The ruins left by the war in Europe and Asia and the rise of the Soviet Union and the Communist threat gave a dramatic and spectacular character to the responsibilities that events imposed on the United States, a country too strong to isolate itself and now aware that its refusal to become involved had helped provoke the war without permitting it to escape from the conflict.

Many of the ideas that had been dominant in the American tradition were not adaptable to the postwar world. The French historian Alexis de Tocqueville had observed that democratic societies tend not to face the possibility of war during peacetime, but think of nothing but war and war alone when the cannons are thundering, as though it were a matter of bringing a task to its end, once and for all, in order to return as quickly as possible to "peaceful works." The United States had devoted itself to this ideal, and in 1945 it still labored under the illusion that the end of the war meant a return to peace and justified demobilization. The Prague coup, the Berlin blockade and, above all, the Korean War dispelled this old illusion. There was no longer any possibility of a radical separation of war and peace, peace without anxieties and war without limits; the paradoxical reality was warlike peace, or the Cold War.

Washington authorities and public opinion were to discover the simple but profound truth of Clausewitz' often misinterpreted maxim—that war is the pursuit of politics by other means. The means of force must remain at all times at the service of politics. Peace without victory is sometimes more fruitful than total victory ratified by unconditional surrender. The defeat of enemy armies is not an end in itself but a means to an end. Even after the beginning of hostilities, statesmen must maintain control of military weapons, leaving to the generals only operational command.

FOR a while the United Nations seemed to Americans to offer a substitute for the old ideologies. Franklin Roosevelt attached vital importance to the United Nations. He was ready to make substantial concessions to Stalin so that the Russian dictator would agree to the creation of an international organization that would replace the League of Nations. Here again the American President was faithful to an American dream: to substitute a rule of

RAYMOND ARON, often called France's foremost political analyst, has become familiar with the U.S. through many trips and visiting professorships. Born in Paris in 1905, he was educated at the University of Paris and the Ecole Normale Supérieure.

At present he is Professor of Sociology at the Sorbonne and chief columnist for *Le Figaro*, a major Paris newspaper. Among his main works published in the United States are *The Century of Total War*, *The Opium of the Intellectuals* and *The Great Debate*.

law for the traditional practices of diplomacy, to submit international relations to legal rules comparable to those that assure civil peace within a nation's own borders.

But experience became an unmerciful teacher. By using the right of veto, the Soviet Union paralyzed the Security Council. Subversive methods undercut the principle of noninterference in other countries' internal affairs—a principle that had constituted the fundamental theory of the United Nations Charter. The United States has nonetheless remained loyal, in words at least, to the United Nations, even though that organization, despite the fact that it has rendered service on a number of occasions, has not fundamentally changed the nature of international relations and does not guarantee security for all. The United States has reluctantly learned that it is weapons, alliances and the balance of power which still dominate the international system, changed as it is.

THE uniqueness of today's international system is due to three characteristics of our age which I will summarize with three adjectives: *planetary, nuclear* and *revolutionary.* Means of production, of destruction and of communication have brought the continents closer together and given them a historic unity. Just as the United States in war had two fleets, one in the Pacific and one in the Atlantic, and two armies, one in Europe, the other in Asia, so the United States has in peace adopted a planetary stance—looking in turn, according to the shifts in the Cold War, toward Saigon or Berlin. The emergence of new nations has rendered the world even more complex and made obsolete the concept of a world divided solely into two contending blocs. The concept of opposition between a developed Northern Hemisphere and an undeveloped Southern has become fashionable. Leopoldville and Jakarta interest the State Department no less than the ancient capitals of Europe and Asia. There is, so to speak, no area on earth to which American diplomacy is indifferent. The planet Earth has become an immense sound box. The political regime of some obscure African republic may be of minor importance now, but that same country could become the center from which the ideas and militants of a pro-Chinese subversion movement might spread in all directions. The popular images of the "snowballing"

of events, of the "domino effect," illustrate the abstract idea that each country is willy-nilly a part of universal history.

Such planetary extension of the international system obliges American diplomacy to disperse its attention and resources over innumerable theaters of operation. Nuclear weapons add another dimension: bombers and ballistic missiles make it possible to bring an unprecedented power of destruction to bear on a given situation anywhere in the world almost instantaneously. A ballistic missile covers thousands of miles in half an hour. The potential danger is everywhere and is constant.

In fact, this danger has temporarily, and for all practical purposes, been reduced to a degree that is compatible with some sort of stability. But another kind of instability defies the efforts of the diplomats: the revolutionary forces that currently grip the world. The revolt of peoples first against colonialism and second against poverty and ineffectual or reactionary governments has created inextricable ties between the internal struggles within nations and the rivalries among nations and among blocs. The violence brought about by the population explosion, by the resistance on the part of the privileged to necessary changes, and by the coexistence on the same planet of developed and underdeveloped countries was not originated by Moscow or Peking, but the parties dedicated to the Marxist-Leninist cause endeavor to control popular movements and to place their men in key positions. The Cuban revolution was not the work of the Communist Party. It was, so to speak, shrewdly taken over by Fidel Castro and his henchmen (some of whom were Communists), and it ended with the country under the control of a socialist regime that declares its allegiance to Marxism-Leninism.

THE character of the international situation has caused American diplomacy to adopt certain objectives over the past 20 years: (1) to check the spread of the U.S.S.R. and of Communism; (2) to prevent nuclear war; and (3) to encourage the liberation and the development of the "third world" of the uncommitted countries. The United States has tried to attain this last objective without causing major conflicts with the European states that in 1945 were the mother countries of colonial empires, without supporting conservative regimes and without giving the Communists the chance to gain power.

During the first phase of the postwar period Europe was or seemed to be the principal theater of diplomatic operations. After 1947 and the beginning of the Marshall Plan the goal of American diplomacy was the economic reconstruction of Western Europe, the reconciliation and even unification of countries recently at war with one another, and the establishment of a collective defense organization that would deter any Soviet aggression. These goals have been achieved: today Europe on the western side of what used to be called—and in the United States is still called—the Iron Curtain is bursting with prosperity after the longest period of continuous and rapid economic growth in its history. The Communist Parties of France and Italy are still large and powerful, especially Italy's; but the threat of foreign aggression as well as of internal subversion, although not entirely gone, has been at least greatly reduced.

But the success of the United States in this regard seems limited, for two reasons. In spite of proposals for the rollback of Communism, American diplomacy has not ceased to be defensive. It has not seriously tried to "liberate" the states of Eastern Europe. When the Soviets suppressed the Hungarian revolution the U.S. was content to make futile and solemn protests and appeals to the United Nations, both steps having no other function than to camouflage passiveness. (In the case of the Anglo-French expedition to Suez, American diplomacy acted in a quite different and efficient way.) Moreover, the reconstruction of Western Europe and the establishment of the European Economic Community, while solving certain problems, created others. The successes of yesterday have been masked by the crises of today.

DURING the early postwar years, when the United States was either alone in possession of the atom bomb or when the Soviet Union had but a limited capacity for retaliation against United States territory, nuclear strategy as officially proclaimed by American generals and politicians was one of massive retaliation. If the Soviet Army ever crossed over certain lines, the Strategic Air Command would go into action and would inflict mortal punishment on the aggressor.

This doctrine never had to be applied. In Europe the line was clearly drawn and respected. In Korea a demarcation line was crossed by the North Korean Army, but that crossing obviously did not warrant an atomic war. What use would it have been to punish the executor while sparing the instigator? And how could the instigator have been punished without spreading the war?

Advances in nuclear weapons and in the means of delivering them, as well as studies pursued in schools and universities and other institutions, resulted, on the arrival of John F. Kennedy at the White House and Robert S. McNamara at the Pentagon in 1961, in the present concept of a "controlled use of force" and the "flexible response," together with a stress on what is called "arms control": a slowdown of the qualitative arms race, cessation of nuclear testing, and efforts to prevent the dissemination of atomic weapons.

THE realization on the part of both great powers that they did not wish to be involved in a war of mutual annihilation (a realization that came slowly and was already visible in 1956 at the time of the double crises of Hungary and the Suez Canal) had an increasing influence on American diplomacy and contributed to a subtle transformation of the international climate in the early 1960s. Of course the two powers remain rivals, but they are also allied in their mutual hostility to the growth of the atomic club, being more anxious to avoid the risk of war than to support the secondary claims of one or another of their allies.

The strategy of arms control was a partial success, especially after the Cuban crisis of 1962. The Soviet leaders seemed for the first time impressed by American resolution, and they consented to an agreement, the significance of which is above all symbolic, on the cessation of aboveground nuclear testing. A few days of acute crisis accomplished what years of negotiations had been unable to do: the Russians agreed to sign a treaty with their enemy at the risk of exasperating their Chinese allies.

At that time, it is true, the Soviet Union and Communist China were already engaged in their historic quarrel. The origin and point of that quarrel were of course the direction of the international Communist movement, the strategy to be adopted by the Marxist-Leninist bloc with respect to the

West, the interpretation of mutually shared doctrine and, at bottom, the divergence of certain national interests. In signing the Moscow Treaty the Soviet leaders resigned themselves to making public the great split inside the Marxist-Leninist world and to an admission of the fact that they no longer hoped for a reconciliation. The fall of Khrushchev changed nothing in this respect.

THE partial rapprochement between the United States and the Soviet Union and the conflict between the latter and Communist China added to the complexity of the international system. Only in Europe—and even there some qualifications have to be made—was it possible to identify the Western camp with democratic regimes and to equate the diffusion of Communism with the expansion of Soviet power. In other parts of the world the confrontation has never been that clear. The United States has been obliged to support undemocratic governments because they were, or seemed to be, the only alternatives to a rise to power by Communist Parties. The White Paper published by the State Department on the eve of the Mao Tse-tung victory was a merciless condemnation of the regime of an allied country. On the other hand, after the death of Stalin and the easing of Soviet diplomacy, American diplomacy, too, had to accept with good grace the neutrality or noninvolvement of old and new nations situated outside the area covered by the Atlantic pact. The Kremlin no longer denounced as imperialist agents the rulers of India or other countries that declared themselves uncommitted. John Foster Dulles and his successors no longer denounced the immorality of neutrality.

On occasion the Soviet Union and the United States even have agreed to accept the noninvolvement of a given country—India for instance, which is receiving or buying both Russian and American arms. From neither side can be heard the proclamation: "Whoever is not with me is against me." Socialist Yugoslavia continues to receive American aid even though it has achieved a reconciliation with the Soviet Union without, however, having rejoined the Soviet camp. Even Poland, which has never left the Soviet bloc, benefits from American aid.

Other approaches have been required in other parts of the world. The predominant concern on the part of American diplomats in Latin America as well as in Africa and Asia is still to be able to prevent the rise to power of a Marxist-Leninist party. At the same time, the U.S.'s realistic (and generous) aim of encouraging economic development and political democracy has not been abandoned. But depending on local circumstances or the preferences of the occupant of the White House or his advisers, American diplomacy has put the accent on the necessity of social reform (this was Kennedy's tendency) or, in fact if not in words, has supported any established government that has a chance of holding on and which is not suspect of Communism.

With respect to the old European empires, American opinion—both that of the diplomats and that of the man in the street—has always been pleased to place itself in the "progressive camp." As the old empires waned, America, born of a liberating revolution, felt close to the people who were waging wars of national liberation, even though the Vietnamese or Algerian revolts against the French may have had nothing in common with the revolt of the American colonies against the British Crown. But this meant that during the whole decolonization period American diplomacy walked a tightrope, berated by one country after another but shrewd and lucky enough not to break either with its European allies (like France) or with the governments of the new states. The crisis set off by the Suez expedition put to a severe trial this irritating and inevitable double game. Once again the irreparable was avoided, mostly because an important segment of French and British opinion condemned the attempt to liquidate Nasser and Nasserism by force.

IT would not be wrong to say that American diplomacy succeeded: torn between the principle of anticolonialism and its European alliances, it won itself the gratitude of neither the liberated peoples nor the defenders of European empires; but at least it avoided the disasters that awaited it on both sides. But here again, such success is partial, and in certain respects it leaves a bequest of still more difficult problems.

The United States is pictured by Marxist-Leninist propaganda as the principal enemy and as the incarnation of capitalist imperialism. Racist South Africa and a Portugal resolved to defend its colonial empire to the end have offered, and continue to offer, targets for the anger, whether spontaneous or manipulated, of the uncommitted nations of the world, of darker-skinned peoples and of the Communists themselves. But more and more it is the United States that is condemned to the role of scapegoat, the epitome of imperialism.

In Vietnam, the U.S. has replaced France as the villain. The United States has sought—but not found—effective officials who would be capable, with U.S. aid, of preventing a Communist take-over. And in Vietnam the U.S. has endeavored, by the limited use of military weapons, to contain China and convert it to a policy of peaceful coexistence.

IN Latin America the United States is the dominant power, although it has no empire there in the European sense of the word. It has invested important sums of money in the region, and in it American corporations are exploiting natural resources, such as oil, tin and coffee. Students and intellectuals tend to confuse hegemony with imperialism; they confuse the development of natural resources with exploitation of the people. The United States is deemed imperialistic if it aids despotic governments; it is also imperialistic if it tries to promote reforms; it is guilty if it supports, or appears to be supporting, men currently in power, and guilty also if, in the interests of the Alliance for Progress, it intervenes in the internal affairs of a state. Whatever it does is wrong.

Moreover, now that the other members of NATO are rid of their empires and thereby acquitted of the crime of colonialism, they sometimes adopt toward American actions in Southeast Asia and Latin America the attitude of indifference or even discreet (or not so discreet) reprobation, which was the attitude of the United States itself a number of years ago toward Holland in Indonesia and France in Indochina and North Africa. Gaullist France goes further; it does not hesitate to condemn "American neocolonialism" and to denounce "the hegemonies" it claims are exerted by the U.S. and the Soviet Union. American public opinion protests that such criticisms are unjust. In the American interpretation of history there is nothing in common between the first and the second Vietnamese wars, between the French defense of the empire and American support of the South Vietnamese Governments. But the Communist and Left-Wing interpretation of history is quite different, and the American effort to

maintain in Saigon regimes judged unworthy is ranked with the French effort between 1946 and 1954. Even without subscribing to the Marxist or Left-Wing line of thought, the significance of the American effort is compromised by the weakness, instability and corruption of the South Vietnamese Governments. Between the French expeditionary corps at grips with the Vietminh and the American troops at grips with the Vietcong, the Vietnamese are likely to notice a similarity.

It is difficult to render a balance sheet on American policy in the uncommitted countries because objectives have not been as clearly defined as in Europe. Most of the new states brought into being by the breakup of European empires declared themselves uncommitted. Many are Socialist, and only North Vietnam and Cuba are frankly Marxist-Leninist. Some observers are pessimistic, however: they believe that there are no game preserves left and that Western influence is everywhere being contested or driven back by Soviet and Chinese influence; in the Near East as in Latin America, both the ideas and those dedicated to the Marxist-Leninist cause are present and active. The competition for the allegiance of the uncommitted countries reaches all continents and takes place on all planes: intellectual, economic, political. But the optimistic observer will reply that this evolution was determined in advance and that the very limitation of defeat is in itself a sort of victory for the U.S. The Europeans departed from their colonial empires but without the Russians and Chinese replacing them. Guinea, after its rupture with France, declared itself Socialist but was disappointed by those to whom it had appealed; without giving up Socialism, Guinea is taking care not to go over to the camp of Soviet Russia or China. Cuba's example has been followed by no other Latin American country. The area of economic underdevelopment and political chaos is expanding more than is the Communist zone.

THE Cold War has not been won and cannot be won. A battle is won: up until now wars, in the old sense of the word, were but battles in the course of international relations. But the Cold War is a long era in the history of mankind; successes in it are provisional and precarious, as defeats in it are partial and reversible. The greatest defeat suffered by the United States was the rise to power of Mao Tse-tung and his henchmen in China. Less than 20 years later this so-called Soviet victory had resulted in the break-up of the Communist bloc, the end of unity in the Marxist-Leninist movement and, as an aftereffect, a growing autonomy for the countries of Eastern Europe. These are at least partial defeats for the Communist camp. Was Stalin making a mistake, from his own standpoint, in negotiating with Chiang Kai-shek and contemplating with a sort of uneasiness the establishment of a Communist regime in China?

HERE arises the major question of this essay: after a generation of experience in world diplomacy has the United States completed its apprenticeship and is it better equipped today to fulfill its responsibilities?

American public opinion and leaders have lost many of their illusions. The crusading spirit has died out. In 1917 the United States entered the war in a great glow of mass enthusiasm to make the world safe for democracy. From the postwar disappointments emerged a new isolationism. Then a new idealism came in World War II: General Eisenhower called his war memoirs *Crusade in Europe*. The setbacks after World War II gave rise not to a revival of isolationism but to pactomania, the anti-Communist obsession: a worldwide operation to hold in check Soviet expansion and to construct a new international order. What is the American reaction to the disappointments of the Cold War and to an ambiguous situation? The reaction is apparently moderate; the country and its leaders seem to be resigned to the frustrations of a war of indefinite duration in which the only hope of victory could be described as the absence of defeat.

The illusion of American omnipotence, to employ the expression of Sir Denis Brogan, is dead. China was not "lost" by the Democratic Administration; the Americans were quite simply powerless to prevent the Communist victory. The schism between Moscow and Peking was not caused by American diplomacy, although American policy of not acknowledging Communist China's claims and of supporting Chiang Kai-shek militarily against attacks on the islands of Quemoy and Matsu in 1958 probably contributed to the Sino-Soviet quarrel. And American diplomacy will not succeed in preventing the dissemination of nuclear arms, for history has shown that no state willingly gives up the right to

weapons that it considers to be crucial for its security.

At the same time, in discovering a common interest with the Soviet Union, the United States lost its "absolute enemy." Evidently China could replace the Soviet Union as the absolute enemy, but public opinion, exposed as it has been to the shock of too many reversals, is threatened by a certain skepticism that would recently have been deemed cynicism. West Germany has become the most faithful European ally; Japan, as General MacArthur so candidly stated to Congress, is now on the right side of the fence, while China, for so many years an object of sympathy for the American people, has moved to the other side.

Stripped of the illusion of omnipotence, with no further crusading spirit, American diplomacy must become used to the desire for independence on the part of its NATO partners. France, under General de Gaulle, expresses this desire most clearly, but with or without de Gaulle the world has changed. Western Europe is still protected by American military power and by itself would be no match for Soviet power. However, Western Europe no longer fears Soviet attack, and because of that it does not feel obliged to follow American leadership. Neither the Atlantic pact nor the common interests that link the Old World with the New will disappear, but a new period has opened in which the defensive passwords of yesterday—like "containment" or "Common Market"—no longer suffice.

UP to now American policy in Europe has been devoted solely to maintaining a status quo of frontiers and to working for the development of economic prosperity and political unity in the region west of the Iron Curtain. The demands for free elections in East Germany were a sort of diplomatic ritual. The division of Germany was morally objected to but accepted in fact. This policy, completed by the recent Soviet-American agreements limiting the testing of nuclear weapons, is perhaps the only realistic one at present. However, the growing independence of the Eastern European countries, the German demands for reunification and the French schemes for a united Europe no longer permit the Americans to pursue their former negative tactics, which are criticized because of their success.

The uncommitted countries find fault with American policy and will continue to do so whether it succeeds or fails. The richest and most powerful country in the world cannot be popular, and the United States in this century must be even more unpopular than Great Britain was in the last century, both for what it is and for what it does. The ruling state is denied what it most wants, and above all the Americans want to be liked. The Soviet Union proclaims all over the world an ideology to which millions of partisans adhere with idealism or fanaticism. The Soviet—or Chinese—supporters are inspired by revolutionary sentiments and the hope of a brilliant future. There is no "American Party" in the uncommitted countries, and although the integrity and impartiality of many opponents of Communism cannot be doubted, it is unavoidable that the privileged classes and the money-minded are attracted to the capitalist cause. Many students and intellectuals all over the world judge the United States unfavorably by the faults of its followers.

THE fact is that American ideologies cannot be transferred. The stability of the American form of government is not due to the multiplicity of parties, trade unions, assemblies and boards of inquiry. The compatibility of freedom with competition and with economic efficiency is assured by respect for the rules of the game, by civic responsibility and by agreement on the basic values. These same institutions, when transplanted to another country, often fail to take root. Despots take over, and despotism without ideology often has the disadvantages of totalitarianism without its advantages.

A further impediment is that the United States makes no attempt to hide its faults. American press services send all over the world pictures of police dogs being used against Negro demonstrators in the South. Crime and violence, the seamy side of American society, are known, shown and published repeatedly everywhere. The Soviet and Chinese societies are hidden, and what they show is a mixture of what they would like to be and what they really are—in other words, a blend of their society as it should be, based on their ideology, and the reality.

A final hindrance to American diplomatic success is that the Americans themselves, when they live abroad, often cut themselves off from the local population by their standard of living and their consumer habits, which can be satisfied only by imported American goods. It is not necessary to mention the extreme cases as described in the well-known book *The Ugly American*. The American Way of Life attracts the masses, but few countries are rich enough to adopt American standards of living. As for the intellectuals, their reasons for disliking American goals and standards often have nothing to do with the Marxism they clamor for, but rather with a nostalgia for the old, aristocratic values and a repugnance for mass culture.

Nevertheless, it would be a mistake to think that the anti-American feeling that exists to a greater or lesser degree in every country is a vital factor in world politics or that it proves the failure of American diplomacy. The importance of the role of the United States in world politics must inevitably give rise to contradictory reactions. The students who demonstrate outside American embassies are possibly the most eager to visit Harvard or Columbia. A French revolutionary once said that one does not reign innocently, and the most powerful state never seems innocent. Everything has a price, especially power and wealth.

The United States has not yet finished its task. Europe is still divided, Communism has not been defeated, hundreds of millions go hungry, the international system has not been stabilized, and countries continue to flout the law. Possibly, however, the Americans are now prepared to admit that certain tasks are by definition never completed. A technician can solve a problem and a judge can render a verdict. Communism, underdevelopment and the Chinese revival are not "problems" that American technicians can solve, and German unity is not a legal case between the Bonn and East German Governments, to be judged by an impartial court. Technical and legal thinking about foreign relations is slowly giving way to thinking historically.

A CONSCIOUSNESS of history does not doom us to despair. We can still keep the hope of an international order that would not be based on the threat of atomic retaliation. History teaches us the virtue of patience and the precariousness of solutions imposed by force. Even the most powerful state has to recognize the limits of its power. All nations belong to the same world and will build together, by cooperation and conflicts, their common future—which will not fulfill completely the aspirations of any one of them.

In the bleak atmosphere of a squalid, garbage-littered courtyard in Harlem, four young ghetto residents while away the hours.

The Pressing Problems of Race and Poverty

While endeavoring to maintain its position as a bulwark of the Free World, the nation has continued to seek solutions to long-standing problems at home. Of these, by far the most critical is that of race. A century after emancipation, many American Negroes are still strangers in their own land. Their unemployment rate is double that of whites, their schooling is poorer, and millions of them live in noxious slums. In the mid-1960s these slums exploded into violence. Although much racial progress had already been won through peaceful pressure, it was not enough: a clear cry from the streets had been sounded. How the U.S. answered the cry might well determine the future of American democracy.

VIOLENCE BORN OF DESPAIR has increasingly plagued the nation's cities

THE RACIAL NIGHTMARE is symbolized by the searching of three Negroes by National Guardsmen during the 1967 rioting in Newark, New Jersey. The Newark eruption, lasting six days, was only one of several major disturbances in urban ghettos that summer. Although most whites expressed shock at the outbreaks, a presidential commission several months later ascribed the underlying cause of the unrest to "white racism," a pervasive, instinctive feeling of superiority over blacks.

GREATER ACHIEVEMENTS by Negro leaders help give their people cause for hope

SENATOR from Massachusetts, Edward W. Brooke *(left)* greets a voter during the campaign that made him the first Negro ever elected to the U.S. Senate by popular vote. A Republican moderate, Brooke is considered by some black militants to be too "middle class" to speak for the ghetto Negro.

JUSTICE of the Supreme Court, Thurgood Marshall stands with his family before the Court building in Washington. The son of a dining car steward, Marshall had been a civil rights lawyer and U.S. Solicitor General. In 1967 he became the first Negro to sit on the nation's highest tribunal.

MAYOR of Cleveland, Ohio, Carl Stokes *(left)* walks with his wife in a snowstorm on the way to the 1967 voting that resulted in his election as the first Negro mayor of a large U.S. city. On the same day another Negro, reformer Richard Hatcher, was chosen mayor of racially tense Gary, Indiana.

Appendix

HISTORICAL DATES

c.50,000-20,000 B.C.	First migrants from Asia, the ancestors of the Indians, reach North America
c.1000 A.D.	Leif Ericson discovers Vinland, possibly New England
1497	John Cabot explores the North American coast
1513	Juan Ponce de León discovers Florida
1565	Spaniards found first permanent colony at St. Augustine (Fla.)
1607	Jamestown Colony founded in what the colonists call Virginia
1619	First legislative body meets in Virginia. First African Negroes sold in Virginia
1620	Mayflower Compact; Pilgrims found Plymouth
1626	Dutch settle New Amsterdam
1643	The New England Confederation unites the colonies of Massachusetts Bay, Plymouth, New Haven and Connecticut
1647	Rhode Island's General Assembly convenes; adopts liberal constitution, including the separation of church and state
1652	Pine Tree shilling minted in Boston in defiance of English law
1673	French explorers Marquette and Joliet sail down the Mississippi
1682	La Salle reaches the mouth of the Mississippi and claims Louisiana for France
1690-1700	Importation of slaves greatly increases, reaching a peak a century later
1700-1735	Shipbuilding becomes a major industry in New England
1720-1730	Whaling industry begins to flourish in New England, reaching a peak a century later
1744-1754	Pennsylvanians and Virginians begin to move westward into Ohio River valley
1764	St. Louis founded by the French
1765	The Stamp Act, the first direct levy on America, passed by British Parliament. Stamp Act Congress meets in New York City to organize resistance
1766	The Sons of Liberty clash with British troops in New York
1767-1771	Daniel Boone explores Kentucky
1770	The Boston Massacre, followed in 1773 by the Boston Tea Party
1774	British Parliament passes Intolerable Acts, uniting the colonies in resistance. First Continental Congress meets
1775	Second Continental Congress meets. Minutemen fight British at Lexington and Concord
1776	Congress adopts Declaration of Independence. Washington retreats from New York across New Jersey but wins at Trenton
1777	Major British defeat at Saratoga. American Army winters at Valley Forge
1778	Franco-American alliance formed
1779-1780	Congress begins debate on peace terms; war continues
1781	Articles of Confederation ratified
1782-1783	Peace talks begin in Paris. British Army surrenders at Yorktown. Americans and British sign final treaty
1785	Indian tribes cede Ohio lands
1787	Constitutional Convention meeting in Philadelphia drafts federal Constitution
1787-1788	State ratifying conventions adopt the Constitution
1789	Federal Government organized in New York; George Washington inaugurated President
1790	First U.S. census reports a total of 3,929,000 inhabitants
1791	Bill of Rights adopted. Vermont becomes the 14th state
1793	Washington issues proclamation of neutrality in the war between France and Britain. Eli Whitney invents cotton gin
1800	National capital transferred to Washington, D.C.
1803	Louisiana Purchase bought from France for about $12 million
1804-1806	Lewis and Clark Expedition to explore the Louisiana Purchase
1812-1814	War with Britain. British occupy Washington, D.C.
1814	Treaty of Ghent restores peace
1817-1825	Construction of Erie Canal
1820	Missouri Compromise prohibits slavery in Louisiana Purchase north of 36° 30'. Missouri becomes a state in 1821
1823	Monroe Doctrine proclaims the American continents are no longer open to new European colonizing
1827-1838	First of great Irish and German migrations to U.S.
1828	Doctrine of Nullification, which holds that states can overrule federal laws, reopens the conflict over federal and state sovereignty. Construction begins on Baltimore and Ohio R.R.
1829	Inauguration of President Andrew Jackson symbolizes triumph of common man
1830	Indian Removal Act to resettle eastern Indians in Oklahoma Territory
1831	Jerome Case founds his thresher works, eventually the world's largest
1832-1835	Nathaniel J. Wyeth opens western part of Oregon Trail. Joseph R. Walker opens Yosemite Valley. Captain Benjamin L. E. Bonneville leads expedition into the Rockies
1834	Cyrus McCormick takes out first patent on reaper. Thomas Davenport invents electric motor
1834-1837	First national labor organization, the National Trades Union
1835	Samuel Colt patents revolver
1835-1836	Texas War of Independence
1837	U.S. recognizes the Republic of Texas. John Deere makes the steel plow. Samuel F.B. Morse invents the telegraph
1841	Overland migration to California begins
1842-1843	Large-scale migration to Oregon
1844	First commercial treaty with China signed. Goodyear perfects the vulcanization of rubber
1846-1848	War with Mexico
1847	The Mormons reach Utah
1848	First Chinese arrive in California. Gold rush to California begins
1849-1850	California draws up a constitution prohibiting slavery and is admitted to the Union. Fugitive Slave Act puts cases involving slaves under federal jurisdiction
1851	Irish immigration reaches peak. The federal Government grants land to the Illinois Central, beginning a policy that spurs railroad growth
1852	Elisha Graves Otis perfects first passenger elevator
1853	Gadsden Purchase, negotiated with Mexico, completes U.S. boundaries
1855	Soo Canal between Lakes Superior and Huron opened
1856	John Brown massacres proslavery settlers at Pottawatomie, Kans.
1857	The Dred Scott Case: Negro Dred Scott denied an appeal by the Supreme Court on the grounds that Negroes are not citizens and cannot sue in the courts
1858	Lincoln-Douglas debates. First stagecoach to West Coast from St. Louis
1859	John Brown's raid on Harpers Ferry. Gold rushes in Colorado and Nevada. First petroleum well at Titusville, Pa.
1860	Lincoln elected President. South Carolina secedes from Union
1861	Confederate Constitution framed. Jefferson Davis elected President of Confederate States. Southern forces fire on Fort Sumter. First Battle of Bull Run. Telegraph links West and East Coasts
1862	Lincoln issues the Emancipation

Proclamation. Homestead Act passed. Battles of Shiloh, Antietam and Fredericksburg

1863 Vicksburg campaign. Battle of Gettysburg

1864 Grant takes command of Union armies. Wilderness campaign. Atlanta campaign; Sherman's march to the sea

1865 Lee surrenders at Appomattox. Lincoln assassinated

1866 Ku Klux Klan organized in Tennessee. Cyrus Field lays first successful transatlantic cable

1867 U.S. purchases Alaska from Russia for $7.2 million. Reconstruction Acts passed

1869 Wyoming passes first U.S. women's suffrage law. First transcontinental railroad completed

1875-1876 Sioux War; Custer and his men wiped out at Little Bighorn

1876 Alexander Graham Bell patents the telephone

1878 Thomas A. Edison patents the phonograph

1879 Edison perfects the first practical incandescent lamp

1880 First major gold strike in Alaska. U.S. surpasses Great Britain in steel production

1884 Ottmar Mergenthaler invents the Linotype

1886 Geronimo's capture marks the end of Plains Indian warfare

1887 Interstate Commerce Commission is set up, the first federal regulatory agency

1889 Oklahoma land rush

1890 Sherman Antitrust Act passed

1891 Edison patents motion-picture camera

1892 Duryea brothers produce their first automobile

1892-1909 Peary explores the Arctic, claiming to reach the North Pole

1893 Henry Ford builds his first car

1894 Federal intervention in the Pullman strike

1896 Supreme Court establishes "separate but equal" doctrine, legalizing segregation

1897-1898 Gold rush in the Klondike

1898 Spanish-American War; Spain cedes Puerto Rico, Guam, Philippines to U.S. for $20 million

1899-1900 Open Door policy in China is adopted

1901 Socialist Party of U.S. organized. Oil discovered in Texas. U.S. Steel Corporation organized

1903 First successful heavier-than-air flight by Wright brothers

1904-1914 Construction of Panama Canal

1905 Formation of Industrial Workers of the World, a militant labor organization

1905-1906 Robert M. LaFollette's Wisconsin reforms set pattern for U.S. progressivism

1907 All-time record for one year's immigration: 1,285,349

1907-1909 As a show of strength the U.S. battle fleet cruises the world

1912 New Mexico and Arizona become states, bringing the number of states to 48

1914 U.S. proclaims its neutrality in World War I. Clayton Antitrust Act. Robert H. Goddard receives first U.S. patent for multistage rockets

1915 German sinkings of *Lusitania* and *Arabic* arouse public sentiment against Germany

1917 U.S. declares war and first U.S. troops begin combat training in France

1918 U.S. troops fight at Château-Thierry and Belleau Wood; join French in Aisne-Marne offensive. The battle of Meuse-Argonne involves 1.2 million U.S. troops. Armistice ends war on Nov. 11

1920 Senate refuses to ratify League of Nations. Women get the vote

1920-1933 Prohibition of domestic sale of intoxicating beverages

1923-1929 "Coolidge Prosperity" marked by Government noninterference with business

1927 Charles A. Lindbergh makes first solo flight from New York to Paris

1928 Al Smith, a Roman Catholic, named Democratic Presidential candidate; loses election to Herbert Hoover

1929 Wall Street crash—beginning of the Great Depression

1931 Hawley-Smoot tariff, highest in U.S. history

1932 The Bonus Army of veterans marches on Washington and is dispersed. Franklin Delano Roosevelt elected President; pledges "New Deal"

1933 Banking panic; U.S. devaluates currency and abandons the gold standard. "First Hundred Days": establishment of New Deal Government agencies and reform legislation

1933-1936 Severe drought turns Great Plains into Dust Bowl

1935-1937 Supreme Court invalidates two of Roosevelt's new Government agencies. Roosevelt tries to "pack the Court" but is defeated in Congress

1937-1938 Sharp recession interrupts gradual business recovery

1938-1940 Roosevelt initiates strong antitrust campaign to wrest economic control from "the few"

1939 Scientists inform Roosevelt of the possibility of making an atom bomb

1940 Destroyers-for-bases deal with Britain. Roosevelt defeats

Wendell Willkie and begins his unprecedented third term

1941 Roosevelt's "Four Freedoms" speech. Lend-lease agreement. Atlantic Charter proclaimed. Japanese attack Pearl Harbor; U.S. declares war on Japan, Germany and Italy

1942 United Nations pact signed by 26 nations. Japanese suffer first major defeat at Midway Island. First self-sustaining nuclear chain reaction achieved

1943-1945 American air power smashes European targets; American naval power sweeps Pacific islands of Japanese invaders

1944 Allied landings in Normandy

1945 Death of Roosevelt. V-E Day on May 8; Germany surrenders. Atom bombs dropped on Hiroshima and Nagasaki. Japan surrenders. San Francisco Conference creates U.N. Charter

1947 Truman Doctrine pledges U.S. to protect Greece and Turkey from Communism in Europe. Marshall Plan implements European recovery

1948-1949 Berlin Airlift

1949 Point Four plan for economic assistance to underdeveloped nations

1950-1954 Korean War involves a total of 1.5 million U.S. troops. Witch hunt of suspected Communists inspired by wild accusations of Senator Joseph R. McCarthy

1952 U.S. announces first successful test of hydrogen bomb

1954 Supreme Court declares "separate but equal" school facilities unconstitutional. U.S.S. *Nautilus*, first atomic-powered submarine, commissioned

1957 Race riots in Little Rock, Ark.

1958 First American artificial satellite is orbited. Commercial jet service begins

1959 Alaska and Hawaii become states

1962 John H. Glenn Jr. becomes first American to orbit earth. Russian missiles withdrawn from Cuba after firm stand by President Kennedy

1963 U.S., Russia and Britain sign nuclear test ban treaty. President Kennedy assassinated

1964 Civil Rights Act goes into effect

1965 President Johnson's Great Society implemented by a flood of legislation. U.S. military support of South Vietnamese Government greatly increased

1968 The Reverend Dr. Martin Luther King Jr., Nobel Peace Prize winner and leader of nonviolent civil rights movement, is shot to death

1968 The United States and North Vietnam begin peace talks in Paris

FAMOUS UNITED STATES CULTURAL FIGURES

LITERATURE

Anne Bradstreet	c.1612-1672	Early colonial poet whose naïve works are often touching
Edward Taylor	c.1644-1729	An immigrant from England, Taylor became the finest 17th Century American poet
Cotton Mather	1663-1728	Powerful Boston clergyman and religious writer; the literary leader of colonial Puritan America
Jonathan Edwards	1703-1758	Severely intellectual New England divine who fought a growing worldliness by preaching a strict Calvinism. *A Careful . . . Inquiry into the Modern Prevailing Notions of . . . Freedom of Will*
Benjamin Franklin	1706-1790	A witty, lucid, economical prose stylist seen at his best in his *Autobiography*
Thomas Paine	1737-1809	Brilliant polemicist whose pleas for liberty did much to shape the thinking of the new nation
Washington Irving	1783-1859	Sophisticated man of letters who wrote many biographies and histories but is best known for his fables of the Catskills ("Rip Van Winkle") and his burlesque *History of New York*
James Fenimore Cooper	1789-1851	Novelist who made popular the wilderness and its pioneers and Indians. *The Last of the Mohicans*
William Cullen Bryant	1794-1878	Poet and editor whose activities gave new dignity and confidence to U.S. letters although his own works tended to be rather pallid. "Thanatopsis"; "To a Waterfowl"
Ralph Waldo Emerson	1803-1882	Philosopher and poet whose influential essays urged America to be self-reliant in both literature and life. Essays: "Self-Reliance"; "The Over-Soul"; "Nature"; "The American Scholar"
Nathaniel Hawthorne	1804-1864	Quiet, isolated writer who sought in his masterpiece, *The Scarlet Letter,* to plumb the problem of human good and evil. *The House of the Seven Gables*
Henry Wadsworth Longfellow	1807-1882	Conventional although often melodious poet. *The Song of Hiawatha;* "Paul Revere's Ride"
John Greenleaf Whittier	1807-1892	Writer of quiet, modest poems of nature and religious reflection. "Snow-Bound"
Edgar Allan Poe	1809-1849	Brilliant and tormented poet and writer of grotesque short stories; invented the detective story
Henry David Thoreau	1817-1862	Philosophical rebel and pungent prose writer who urged on Americans the virtue of complete personal independence. *Walden;* "Civil Disobedience"; *The Maine Woods*
Herman Melville	1819-1891	Tormented questioner whose masterpiece, *Moby-Dick,* raises the great moral problems and ends by doubting the very order of the universe. *Typee; White-Jacket; Redburn; Pierre; Billy Budd*
Walt Whitman	1819-1892	Pioneering poet who broke totally with the genteel tradition and in his powerful free verse found America's poetic voice. *Leaves of Grass;* "When Lilacs Last in the Dooryard Bloom'd"
Emily Dickinson	1830-1886	Poet-recluse whose superb verse ponders the questions of love, death and evil
Samuel Langhorne Clemens (Mark Twain)	1835-1910	A spinner of hilarious tall tales, Twain produced one unquestioned masterpiece, *The Adventures of Huckleberry Finn,* in which he entered the realm of myth and epic
William Dean Howells	1837-1920	Realist novelist whose increasingly profound view of life is reflected in his fine later novels
Henry Adams	1838-1918	Profound thinker about the nature of society. *The Education of Henry Adams*
William James	1842-1910	Superb prose stylist who studied and taught physiology and psychology as well as philosophy. A founder of Pragmatism. *The Principles of Psychology; The Varieties of Religious Experience*
Henry James	1843-1916	Profound and prolific novelist whose works examine with sensitivity the deepest moral problems as well as the society of his time. *The Portrait of a Lady; The Ambassadors; The Wings of the Dove*
John Dewey	1859-1952	Distinguished philosopher and highly influential theorist of education. *Democracy and Education*
Edith Wharton	1862-1937	Elegant, humorous novelist of manners. *The Age of Innocence; The Custom of the Country*
George Santayana	1863-1952	Philosopher and literary critic; a precise thinker and elegant prose stylist. "Dickens"; *Character and Opinion in the United States; The Life of Reason*
Edwin Arlington Robinson	1869-1935	Poet whose sense of the tragedy of life is often expressed in dry portraits of Maine types
Frank Norris	1870-1902	Naturalistic novelist who saw society as maliciously destructive. *McTeague; The Octopus; The Pit*
Stephen Crane	1871-1900	Short-lived writer of realistic but haunting short stories (such as "The Blue Hotel") and a fine novel about soldiers in the Civil War, *The Red Badge of Courage*
Theodore Dreiser	1871-1945	Writer of massive, impressive novels in which the heroes and heroines are usually destroyed by the blind forces of society. *Sister Carrie; Jennie Gerhardt; An American Tragedy*
Willa Cather	1874-1947	Accomplished novelist who often wrote of the continent's past. *Death Comes for the Archbishop*
Robert Frost	1874-1963	Poet who, in his best poems, used comfortable country images to spell out most uncomfortable truths. A profound, tough-minded artist. *Collected Poems*
Wallace Stevens	1879-1955	Brilliant poetic craftsman whose poems generally seek to define the nature of reality
H(enry) L(ouis) Mencken	1880-1956	Savage critic of what he considered the worst fatuities of the American scene: *Prejudices.* Became a great philologist: *The American Language.* Autobiography: *Newspaper Days*
William Carlos Williams	1883-1963	Poet who wrote delicate but strong verse evoking the U.S. scene. *Collected Poems; Paterson*
Ring Lardner	1885-1933	Mordantly funny short stories that perfectly capture American speech. *You Know Me, Al; How to Write Short Stories; Round Up*
Ezra Pound	1885-	Poet whose influence on other writers is perhaps as important as his own work. The Cantos
Marianne Moore	1887-	Poet whose quiet, feminine verse puts her among America's leading writers. *Collected Poems*
Eugene O'Neill	1888-1953	Playwright whose often clumsy but always powerful dramas set a new standard of seriousness for American theater. *Desire Under the Elms; Mourning Becomes Electra*
T(homas) S(tearns) Eliot	1888-1965	Missouri-born poet who became a British citizen; perhaps the most respected and influential poet and critic of the 20th Century. *The Waste Land; Collected Poems; Selected Essays*
John Crowe Ransom	1888-	Poet of expert craftsmanship and an excellent, highly influential literary critic
Conrad Aiken	1889-	An accomplished poet and fiction writer who has been quietly and modestly building up an impressive lifework. Short stories and novels. *Collected Poems*
E(dward) E(stlin) Cummings	1894-1962	Witty as well as romantic poet who praised love in verse that often achieves great lyric beauty
Katherine Anne Porter	1894-	Expert novelist and short-story writer. *Pale Horse, Pale Rider; Flowering Judas; Ship of Fools*
Edmund Wilson	1895-	Forceful, authoritative and often brilliant critic of literature. *Axel's Castle; The Triple Thinkers*
F. Scott Fitzgerald	1896-1940	Uneven but often brilliant novelist of the 1920s. *The Great Gatsby; Tender Is the Night*
John Dos Passos	1896-	Writer of generally pessimistic although lively examinations of life in America. *U.S.A.*
William Faulkner	1897-1962	Great novelist whose saga of his native South, carried forward in many novels and stories, is

	perhaps the most profound exploration of the nature of man written in the U.S. *Light in August; The Sound and the Fury; Absalom, Absalom!;* "The Bear"
Ernest Hemingway	1898-1961

Ernest Hemingway 1898-1961
Nobel Prize winner whose sensitive and powerful early short stories (collected in *In Our Time, Men Without Women, Winner Take Nothing*) are generally considered his best work

Hart Crane 1899-1932
Poet who tried to comprehend in his work his own troubled soul and the beauty and terror of modern industrial America. *The Bridge; Collected Poems*

Allen Tate 1899-
Poet and influential critic who helped launch the "New Criticism." *On the Limits of Poetry*

Nathanael West 1902-1940
Writer of mordant, brilliant short novels. *Miss Lonelyhearts; The Day of the Locust*

Kay Boyle 1903-
Writer of fine, workmanlike short stories that anatomize many of the ills of modern society

Lillian Hellman 1905-
Playwright whose works give a distinctly grim view of human character. *The Little Foxes*

Lionel Trilling 1905-
Highly respected social and literary critic. *Matthew Arnold; The Liberal Imagination*

Robert Penn Warren 1905-
Distinguished critic and poet. *Selected Poems*. Novel: *All the King's Men*

Richard Wright 1908-1960
One of the first Negro writers to speak out honestly about the plight of his race. *Native Son*

Eudora Welty 1909-
Writer of many fine short stories set in the U.S. South. *A Curtain of Green; The Wide Net*

Ralph Ellison 1914-
Critic whose *The Invisible Man* is among the best studies of the situation of the U.S. Negro

Tennessee Williams 1914-
Eloquent and successful playwright whose works usually portray people, families or society in the process of demoralization and decay. *The Glass Menagerie; A Streetcar Named Desire*

Arthur Miller 1915-
Playwright whose works are powerful but too often ponderous. *Death of a Salesman*

Robert Lowell 1917-
Poet whose works investigate the nature of America and his own New England heritage. *Lord Weary's Castle; For the Union Dead*

James Baldwin 1924-
Fine stylist whose essays define the problems of being a Negro in the U.S. *Notes of a Native Son*

Flannery O'Connor 1925-1964
Writer of short stories and novels of her native South that combine wild humor and Gothic horror. *A Good Man Is Hard to Find; The Violent Bear It Away*

PAINTING

John Singleton Copley 1738-1815
One of America's greatest portrait painters. *Paul Revere; Nicholas Boylston*

Charles Willson Peale 1741-1827
A patriot, Peale produced portraits and miniatures of many of the leaders of the American Revolution. *John Adams; John Paul Jones*

Gilbert Stuart 1755-1828
Great portraitist whose beautifully painted works seem to reveal the psychological depths of his sitters. *George Washington; James Monroe; The Skater*

Washington Allston 1779-1843
Romantic painter who suffused his literary and historical subjects with poetic suggestiveness. *Moonlit Landscape*

Thomas Cole 1801-1842
One of the first and finest painters of the Hudson River School: romantic landscapes

George Caleb Bingham 1811-1877
One of the first painters of the West; luminous works showing life on the Mississippi and Missouri Rivers. *The Wood Boat; Fur Traders Descending the Missouri*

James Abbott McNeill Whistler 1834-1903
Boldly experimental painter and meticulous engraver. *An Arrangement in Grey and Black* (erroneously known as "Whistler's Mother"); the "Nocturnes"

Winslow Homer 1836-1910
Painter whose Yankee fidelity to the way things look and early training as a magazine illustrator combined to make his painting both highly dramatic and realistic. *Eight Bells; Gulf Stream*

Thomas Eakins 1844-1916
Increasingly recognized as one of America's greatest painters, Eakins devoted his life to perfecting his technique. *Max Schmitt in a Single Scull; Walt Whitman; The Swimming Hole*

Albert Pinkham Ryder 1847-1917
Painter-recluse who transformed the seascapes of his native New England into brooding, mystical scenes. *Under a Cloud; Toilers of the Sea*

John Singer Sargent 1856-1925
An accomplished painter of portraits and genre pieces. *Henry James; Madame X*

Maurice Prendergast 1859-1924
Quietly avant-garde painter who did masterful watercolors of Italy, the Boston area's beaches and New York's Central Park. *Revere Beach; The Mall, Central Park*

Frederic Remington 1861-1909
Accurate, prolific recorder of the vanishing West in paintings and sculpture

John Marin 1870-1953
Brilliant master of watercolor who combined strong, linear elements with subdued colors to produce near-abstract images of New York City and the Maine coast

John Sloan 1871-1951
Outstanding member of the "Ashcan School" who painted back yards, city streets and common people in a successful revolt against the conservative traditions of academic painting

Marsden Hartley 1877-1943
Early abstract expressionist (*Portrait of a German Officer*) who later turned to more traditional landscapes of his native Maine. *Robin Hood Cove, Georgetown, Maine*

Arthur G. Dove 1880-1946
One of the first Americans to create pure abstractions; employed forms derived from nature

Hans Hofmann 1880-1966
Influential teacher and an important spokesman for the Abstract Expressionist movement

George Bellows 1882-1925
Carrying on the tradition of the Ashcan School, Bellows applied his direct, vigorous realism to dramatic scenes such as prize fights. *Dempsey and Firpo; Stag at Sharkey's*

Edward Hopper 1882-1967
Painter of stark, geometrical oils and watercolors of American buildings, towns and cities with vibrant color and powerful design. *Early Sunday Morning; Gas; Night Hawks*

Charles Sheeler 1883-1965
Realist fond of painting factories and the machinery of the industrial age

Georgia O'Keeffe 1887-
Painter whose works usually focus on a single element in nature and magnify it until the final image is one of pure abstraction. *The White Flower; The Mountain, New Mexico*

Mark Tobey 1890-
Abstract painter of intricately textured canvases. *Universal Field*

Milton Avery 1893-1964
Painter of vibrant and luminous landscapes with large, simplified forms. *Clear Cut Landscape*

Charles Burchfield 1893-1967
Originally a realist, Burchfield later turned to swirling, brilliantly colored plant forms

Stuart Davis 1894-1964
Profoundly influenced by the Armory Show of 1913, Davis worked out his own form of

(Continued on next page)

Cubism. A pioneer in U.S. art. *Egg Beater, Number 2; The Paris Bit; For Internal Use Only*

Reginald Marsh	1898-1954	Realist whose paintings and drawings usually show the seamy side of big-city life and often have a satiric bite. *Why Not Use the "L"*
Ben Shahn	1898-	Painter whose works often protest against the plight of the poor and the greed of the rich
Philip Evergood	1901-	Best known as a painter of social protest: bleak, tragic depictions of the Great Depression
Mark Rothko	1903-	Abstract painter whose works are usually made up of rectangular bands of color so brilliant that the whole canvas seems to breathe and pulsate. *Number 10*
Arshile Gorky	1904-1948	One of the great innovators of 20th Century painting in America, Gorky combined the older forms of abstract art and Cubism with the newer influences of Surrealism
Willem de Kooning	1904-	Bold, articulate member of the Abstract Expressionist or "Action Painting" movement
Clifford Still	1904-	One of the most influential leaders in modern American art: stark, austere canvases
Franz Kline	1910-1962	Action painter whose bold black-and-white paintings seem to evoke the ragged and torn images of contemporary industrial cities. *Wanamaker Block*
Jackson Pollock	1912-1956	Revolutionary painter of the Abstract Expressionist School who relied to a large degree on spontaneous action, dripping brilliant colors on large canvases
Jack Levine	1915-	Painter of satirical canvases that mock big-city graft and other unfortunate aspects of U.S. life. *Gangster Funeral; Election Night*
Robert Motherwell	1915-	Leader of Abstract Expressionism whose early paintings were influenced by Cubism
Andrew Wyeth	1917-	Highly sophisticated technician, at his best doing realistic tempera studies of rural scenes
Theodoros Stamos	1922-	Abstract Expressionist painter; a master of color that shimmers on his canvases
Robert Rauschenberg	1925-	Artist whose work combines such "found objects" as stuffed birds, rope, bottles and mirrors and seems to capture all the effluvium of the modern world

SCULPTURE

Horatio Greenough	1805-1852	Early American sculptor who was also a theorist of functionalism in architecture
Gaston Lachaise	1882-1935	Sculptor of the human body whose massive, rounded forms broke away from the stiff, academic traditions which preceded him. *Standing Woman*
Alexander Archipenko	1887-1964	Innovator in American sculpture whose experiments paralleled those of Constantin Brancusi and Henry Moore in Europe. *Torso in Space*
Alexander Calder	1898-	Inventor of "mobiles" and "stabiles" who has added a new dimension to sculpture
Louise Nevelson	1900-	Daring, inventive sculptor whose works include large walls made of many variously shaped pieces of wood which give the impression of ruins left by an ancient civilization
Isamu Noguchi	1904-	Sculptor who has also worked in the fields of industrial and landscape design. *Humpty Dumpty*
David Smith	1906-1965	Using industrial materials such as iron and stainless steel, Smith revolutionized modern American sculpture with his highly refined, light and airy structures
Theodore Roszak	1907-	Sculptor of semiabstract and powerful images made of cut and welded steel. *Sea Sentinel*
Leonard Baskin	1922-	Sculptor whose brooding images reflect an imagination preoccupied with death

ARCHITECTURE

Benjamin H. Latrobe	1764-1820	One of America's first independent architects who insisted on a rational design reflecting the demands and needs of the young nation. Chiefly responsible for present U.S. Capitol
James Bogardus	1800-1874	Among the first architects to use cast iron as a structural framework, a system that showed the way for the steel construction of the first skyscrapers
William Le Baron Jenney	1832-1907	Innovator in U.S. architecture who used the metal frame and eliminated load-bearing walls
Henry Hobson Richardson	1838-1886	Applied Romanesque style to large buildings, lending grandeur to industrial America
John Wellborn Root	1850-1891	An architect whose vigorous leadership made the Chicago School a decisive center of design
Louis Sullivan	1856-1924	Profoundly influential leader of the Chicago School who concentrated much of his energy on the refinement and clear articulation of the tall frame building
Frank Lloyd Wright	1869-1959	Protégé of Sullivan whose radical pioneering concepts gave U.S. architecture new significance
Ludwig Mies van der Rohe	1886-	Recognized master of metal-and-glass construction; crystalline expressions of rectilinear form
Eero Saarinen	1910-1961	Followed Mies van der Rohe in the precise use of metal and glass and then went on to develop far more radical shapes, employing reinforced concrete, stainless steel and other materials

MUSIC

Lowell Mason	1792-1872	Composer of hymns whose crusade for musical education deeply influenced U.S. culture
Stephen Foster	1826-1864	Composer of universally loved songs. *Old Folks at Home; My Old Kentucky Home*
Edward MacDowell	1861-1908	Pianist-composer whose works reflect both his European training and his love of the American past. First U.S. composer to achieve world recognition
Charles Ives	1874-1954	Daringly experimental composer who used polyrhythm and polytonality long before avant-garde composers of Europe. His works often attempt to convey an American scene
Cole Porter	1893-1964	Prolific composer-lyricist of often dazzlingly clever show tunes
George Gershwin	1898-1937	Composer of original and often moving show tunes with clever lyrics by his brother Ira
Edward Kennedy "Duke" Ellington	1899-	Bandleader and composer who has written some 1,500 jazz tunes for his orchestra and many longer, more complex compositions. *Sophisticated Lady; Black, Brown and Beige*
Aaron Copland	1900-	Important composer who uses themes and techniques derived from folk music and jazz
Samuel Barber	1910-	Widely performed composer of highly lyrical works. *Vanessa; Adagio for Strings*
John Cage	1913-	Outstanding innovator in modern music who employs hitherto unknown sounds and tones

FOR FURTHER READING

Chapter 1: Character of the U.S.

Botkin, B. A., ed., *Sidewalks of America*. Bobbs-Merrill Company, 1954.

Brogan, Denis W., *The American Character*. Alfred A. Knopf, 1956.

Chester, Edward W., *Europe Views America*. Public Affairs Press, 1962.

Gunther, John, *Inside U.S.A.* Harper & Row, 1951.

Lerner, Max, *America As a Civilization*. (2 vols.) Simon and Schuster, 1957.

Lipset, Seymour Martin, *The First New Nation*. Basic Books, Inc., 1963.

Schlesinger, Arthur M., Sr., *Paths to the Present*. Houghton Mifflin, 1964.

White, T. H., *America At Last*. Putnam, 1965.

Chapter 2: History

Alden, John Richard, *The American Revolution: 1775-1783*. Harper & Row, 1954.

Bowers, Claude G., *Jefferson in Power*. Houghton Mifflin, 1936.

Ferrand, Max, *The Framing of the Constitution of the United States*. Yale University Press, 1913.

Fiske, John, *The Critical Period of American History, 1783-1789*. Houghton Mifflin, 1957.

Freidel, Frank, *America in the Twentieth Century*. Alfred A. Knopf, 1960.

Hofstadter, Richard, William Miller, and Daniel Aaron, *The American Republic*. (2 vols.) Prentice-Hall, 1959.

The LIFE History of the United States. Time Inc., 1963-1964.

Miller, John C., *Alexander Hamilton: Portrait in Paradox*. Harper & Row, 1959. *The Federalist Era, 1789-1801*. Harper & Row, 1960.

Morison, Samuel Eliot, *The Oxford History of the American People*. Oxford University Press, 1965.

Chapter 3: The Political System

Beard, Charles A., *American Government and Politics*. Macmillan, 1949.

Beloff, Max, *The American Federal Government*. Oxford University Press, 1959.

Brogan, D. W., *Politics in America*. Harper & Row, 1954.

Bryce, James, *The American Commonwealth*. Putnam, 1959.

Corwin, E. S., *The President: Office and Powers, 1787-1957*. New York University Press, 1957.

Hamilton, Alexander, John Jay, and James Madison, *The Federalist Papers*. New American Library, 1961.

Key, V. O., Jr., *Politics, Parties, and Pressure Groups*. Crowell, 1964.

Laski, Harold J., *The American Democracy*. Viking Press, 1948.

McCloskey, Robert G., *The American Supreme Court*. University of Chicago Press, 1960.

Rossiter, Clinton, *The American Presidency*. Harcourt, Brace & World, 1960.

Tocqueville, Alexis de, *Democracy in America*. Alfred A. Knopf, 1944.

Van Doren, Carl, *The Great Rehearsal*. Viking Press, 1948.

Young, Roland, *The American Congress*. Harper & Row, 1958.

Chapter 4: The Nation's Economy

Barnes, James A., *Wealth of the American People*. Prentice-Hall, 1949.

Berle, Adolf A., Jr., *The American Economic Republic*. Harcourt, Brace & World, 1963.

Bining, Cecil Arthur, and Thomas C. Cochran, *The Rise of American Economic Life*. Scribner's, 1964.

Fainsod, Merle, and Lincoln Gordon, *Government and the American Economy*. Norton, 1948.

Faulkner, Harold Underwood, *American Economic History*. Harper & Row, 1960.

Galbraith, John Kenneth, *The Affluent Society*. Houghton Mifflin, 1958.

Harris, Seymour E., ed., *American Economic History*. McGraw-Hill, 1961.

Krooss, Herman E., *American Economic Development*. Prentice-Hall, 1955.

Mikesell, Raymond F., *United States Economic Policy and International Relations*. McGraw-Hill, 1952.

Nettels, Curtis P., *Emergence of a National Economy, 1775-1815*. Holt, Rinehart & Winston, 1962.

Shannon, Fred Albert, *America's Economic Growth*. Macmillan, 1951.

Soule, George, *Economic Forces in American History*. William Sloane Associates, 1952.

Veblen, Thorstein, *The Theory of the Leisure Class*. Modern Library, 1934.

Chapter 5: The Arts

Barker, Virgil, *American Painting*. Macmillan, 1950.

Burchard, John, and Albert Bush-Brown, *The Architecture of America*. Little, Brown, 1961.

Chase, Gilbert, *America's Music*. McGraw-Hill, 1955.

Ewen, David, *History of Popular Music*. Barnes & Noble, 1961.

Goodrich, Lloyd, and John I. H. Baur, *American Art of Our Century*. Praeger, 1961.

McCallum, Ian, *Architecture U.S.A.* Reinhold, 1959.

Matthiessen, Francis O., *American Renaissance*. Oxford University Press, 1941.

Mellers, Wilfrid, *Music in a New Found Land*. Alfred A. Knopf, 1965.

Miller, Perry, *American Puritans, Their Prose and Poetry*. Doubleday, 1956.

Shapiro, Nat, and Nat Hentoff, eds., *The Jazz Makers*. Rinehart, 1957.

Spiller, Robert E., and others, eds., *Literary History of the United States*. Macmillan, 1964.

Stearns, Marshall W., *The Story of Jazz*. Oxford University Press, 1956.

Trent, William P., and others, eds., *The Cambridge History of American Literature*. Macmillan, 1943.

Ulanov, Barry, *A History of Jazz in America*. Viking Press, 1952.

Chapter 6: The Uses of Leisure

De Grazia, Sebastian, *Of Time, Work, and Leisure*. Twentieth Century, 1962.

Denney, Reuel, *The Astonished Muse*. University of Chicago Press, 1957.

Kaplan, Max, *Leisure in America*. John Wiley & Sons, 1960.

Kerr, Walter, *The Decline of Pleasure*. Simon and Schuster, 1962.

Madow, Pauline, ed., *Recreation in America*. H. W. Wilson, 1965.

Miller, Norman P., and Duane M. Robinson, *The Leisure Age*. Wadsworth, 1963.

Ordway, Samuel H., Jr., *Prosperity Beyond Tomorrow*. Ronald Press, 1955.

Riesman, David, *Abundance for What?* Doubleday, 1964.

Chapter 7: Religion

Berger, Peter L., *The Noise of Solemn Assemblies*. Doubleday, 1961.

Hall, Thomas Cuming, *The Religious Background of American Culture*. Frederick Ungar, 1959.

Herberg, Will, *Protestant-Catholic-Jew*. Doubleday, 1955.

Oaks, Dallin H., ed., *The Wall Between Church and State*. University of Chicago Press, 1963.

Olmstead, Clifton E., *History of Religion in the United States*. Prentice-Hall, 1960.

Rosten, Leo, ed., *A Guide to the Religions of America*. Simon and Schuster, 1963.

Smith, James Ward, and A. Leland Jamison, eds., *Religion in American Life*. Princeton University Press, 1961.

Sperry, Willard L., *Religion in America*. Macmillan, 1946.

Sweet, William W., *The Story of Religion in America*. Harper & Row, 1950.

Chapter 8: Education

Conant, James Bryant, *The American High School Today*. McGraw-Hill, 1959.

Goodman, Paul, *Compulsory Mis-Education*. Horizon Press, 1964.

Hutchins, Robert M., *The Conflict in Education: In a Democratic Society*. Harper & Row, 1953.

Kilpatrick, William H., *Philosophy of Education*. Macmillan, 1951.

Mayer, Martin, *The Schools*. Harper & Row, 1961.

Meyer, Adolphe E., *An Educational History of the American People*. McGraw-Hill, 1957.

Woodring, Paul, *Let's Talk Sense About Our Schools*. McGraw-Hill, 1953.

Chapter 9: The U.S. and the World

Bailey, Thomas A., *A Diplomatic History of the American People*. Appleton-Century-Crofts, 1964.

Carleton, William G., *The Revolution in American Foreign Policy*. Random House, 1963.

Davids, Jules, *America and the World of Our Time*. Random House, 1960.

Marshall, Charles Burton, *The Limits of Foreign Policy*. Henry Holt & Company, 1954.

Rostow, Walt W., *The United States in the World Arena*. Harper & Row, 1960.

Credits

The sources for the illustrations in this book appear below. Credits for pictures from left to right are separated by commas, from top to bottom by dashes.

Cover—Richard Meek
8, 9—Leonard McCombe
13—John R. Freeman
17—Garry Winogrand
18, 19—John Zimmerman
20, 21—George Silk
22, 23—Farrell Grehan
24, 25—A. Y. Owen
26, 27—Fred Lyon from Rapho-Guillumette
28—Richard Meek
33—The Bettmann Archive, Culver Pictures (2), Matthew A. Grady courtesy the University of Washington
37—Declan Haun from Black Star
38, 39—Joern Gerdts, Garry Winogrand—Joern Gerdts, Garry Winogrand
40, 41—Don Cravens, Lee Friedlander
42, 43—Joern Gerdts
44—Richard Meek
45—Declan Haun from Black Star
46, 47—Jon Brenneis—John Zimmerman
48—Marvin E. Newman
53—The Granger Collection
58 through 67—Richard Meek
68—Marvin E. Newman
74—Drawing by Matt Greene
78, 79—Declan Haun from Black Star
80, 81—Alfred Eisenstaedt
82, 83—Declan Haun from Black Star
84, 85—Jon Brenneis
86, 87—Alfred Eisenstaedt

88, 89—Don Cravens
90—David Moore from Black Star photographed at New York State Theater, Lincoln Center for the Performing Arts
94—Culver Pictures
95—The Bettmann Archive
96—Culver Pictures
102—Paul Mayen
103—A. Y. Owen
104—Farrell Grehan—reproduced courtesy of *Art in America* No. Five 1964
105—Herbert Orth courtesy Mr. and Mrs. Arnold Maremont
106, 107—Herbert Orth courtesy The Metropolitan Museum of Art Samuel D. Lee Fund 1934, Fernand Bourges courtesy of the School of Medicine, University of Pennsylvania—George Bellows' *Dempsey and Firpo* 1924 Oil Collection of the Whitney Museum of American Art, New York
108—Fernand Bourges courtesy Mr. and Mrs. Mark Reed, Fernand Bourges courtesy The Fogg Art Museum, Harvard University—Ben Shahn *Portrait of Myself When Young* 1943, photograph by Herbert Orth, Collection The Museum of Modern Art, New York Purchase
109—Collection of Mr. and Mrs. Stanley Marcus, Dallas, Texas—Herbert Orth from a private collection

110—Collection of the Downtown Gallery—William J. Summits courtesy Munson-Williams-Proctor Institute, Utica, New York, Edward W. Root bequest
111—Collection of the Downtown Gallery—Albright-Knox Art Gallery, Buffalo, New York, Gift of Seymour H. Knox
112—Joern Gerdts
121—Steven C. Wilson
122, 123—Leonard McCombe
124, 125—Leonard McCombe except bottom left Arthur Siegel
126, 127—Jon Brenneis
128—Joern Gerdts
129—Steven C. Wilson
130, 131—John Loengard, Leonard McCombe
132, 133—Walter Sanders
137—Courtesy the Chicago Historical Society
141 through 149—Burk Uzzle
150, 151—Francis Miller
156—Drawing by James Flora
159—Gjon Mili
160, 161—Leonard McCombe except top center Ivan Massar from Black Star
162, 163—Leonard McCombe
164 through 167—Don Cravens
168—Jerry A. Rose
177—Gordon Parks
178, 179—James Pickerell
180—Ted Polumbaum—Lee Balterman
181—Henry Grossman

ACKNOWLEDGMENTS

The editors wish to express their thanks to Henry F. Graff, Professor of History, Columbia University, who read and commented in detail on the text, and to Peter B. Kenen, Professor of Economics at Columbia, who read and commented on Chapter 4.

Sigmund Skard, who wrote Chapter 5, wishes to acknowledge his indebtedness to Chester E. Eisinger, Professor of English at Purdue University, and Robert E. Spiller, Professor of English Literature at the University of Pennsylvania.

✕✕✕

Production staff for Time Incorporated

John L. Hallenbeck (Vice President and Director of Production)

Robert E. Foy and Caroline Ferri

Text photocomposed under the direction of

Albert J. Dunn and Arthur J. Dunn

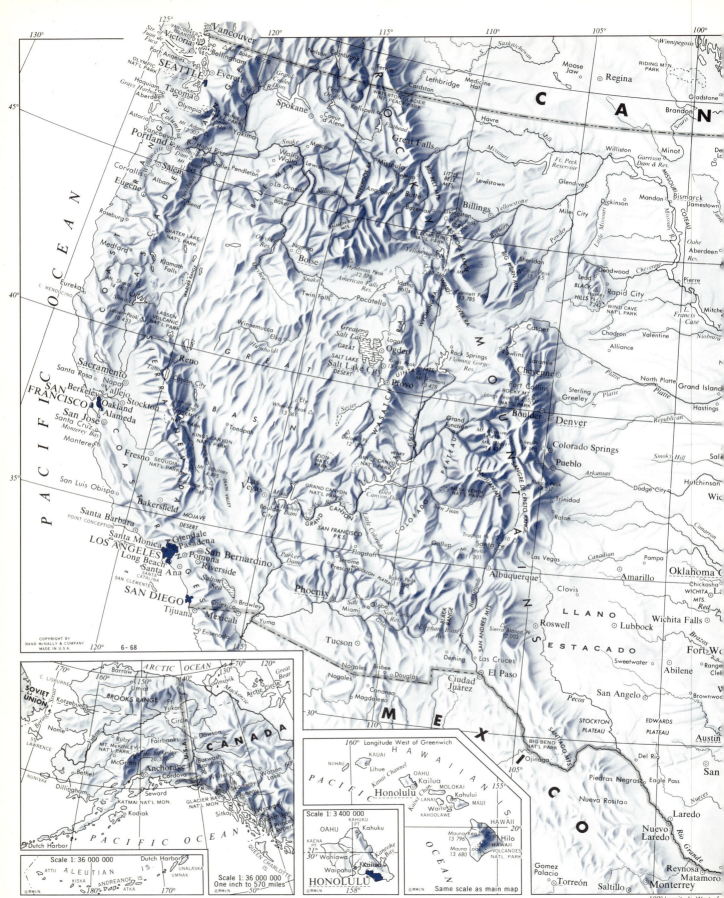